dino fauci's

THE POWER OF PAINT

Personalize Your Environment with
Color & Specialty Finishes

Diane,

May the Colors in your
life always bring
happiness!

Best Always,

Dino

By dino fauci

The Power of Paint

© 2010 dino fauci companies

Printed in the United States of America

Fauci, Dino
     Dino Fauci's The Power of Paint, Personalizing your Environment with Color and Specialty Finishes / by Dino Fauci

Cover by Lex Gable, Dino Fauci and Rashied Williams. Layout by Dino Fauci and Dawn Teagarden. Photos by Lex Gable & Dino Fauci. For information, go to dinofauci.com.

ISBN: 978-0-9843299-1-5

Warning – Disclaimer

This book is dedicated to my father, Chuck for teaching me my work ethic, the value of discipline, responsibility, pride and love of paint.

To my mother, Pat for all of your patience, support, encouragement and appreciation with all that I do.

Because of you two, I am able to enjoy this wonderful journey. My love and appreciation for you both is endless.

"In my two decades of painting, I have never seen anyone with as much expertise in so many areas of painting and design as Dino Fauci...that's why we call him *The Lord of Paint*."

– *Bryan Wallace*

contents

INTRODUCTION 7

PROLOGUE: The Power of "Why?" 11

1 COLOR: What Is Color?.................................19

2 SPECIAL FINISHES: What is a Specialty Finish?.......47

3 ARCHITECTURAL STYLE:
"You Can't Be Something You Are Not!" 81

4 UNDERSTANDING YOUR ENVIRONMENT:
Lighting; Natural & Artificial....................................95

5 IDENTIFYING PROBLEM AREAS:
& Ways To Transform Them...................................103

6 CREATING A THEME: Storytelling 131

7 CLASSICAL VS. TRENDY: Traditional vs. Modern.....141

8 HOME SHOPPING 147

9 DIY: Do It Yourself..161

10 TOOLS AND MATERIALS...177

11 DEALING WITH ARTISTS & CONTRACTORS.............191

12 PREPARING A HOME FOR SALE................................201

WRAP UP 209

ACKNOWLEDGMENTS 211

TESTIMONIALS 217

FAQs: Frequently Asked Questions......................223

GLOSSARY 233

ABOUT THE AUTHOR..245

*Resin cast sculpture faux painted
as white granite.*

INTRODUCTION

"When you open your mind, you allow yourself to see things you've never seen before. When you learn that everything in life is art, you begin to appreciate everything old in a new way."

Welcome to the world of color! Imagination, inspiration and insight combined with use of specialty finishes give everyone the power to transform an environment. Mundane homes and business environments can miraculously become inspiring personalized spaces using the secrets I am about to share with you. Paint, a few simple tools, and the methods in this book, are all that is required to achieve amazing results.

Decades of experience attained over the course of an extremely unique career in traditional painting, specialty painting, and theme park production design, is the foundation of knowledge contained in this book. It will make seemingly complicated techniques available to anyone. All you need is a desire to learn!

One critical step frequently omitted in instructional painting books is the process which leads up to the actual painting. There is far more to choosing and creating a personalized environment with color and specialty finishes, than knowing how to apply paint. How and why colors are chosen is critical. Throughout this book we question each step of a process. Before anything is done, we need to know why it is done. Learning to analyze various options and determining their value in the space are essential to the overall process. This book will aid the reader in discovering the best paint design solution for them.

This book is not only about color and finishes, but about how you see your world. It is about honesty, authenticity and character in design. We will explore how finding what matters most to you and your family is at the heart of the process. It is as much about discovering who you are as it is about applying paint. Using that information to create the environment that truly represents you is the goal of this book. You will, of course, gain professional painting trade secrets which will save time, money and a lot of unnecessary frustration.

"When a space feels good before any furnishings are in place, you know you have created something special."

– Dino Fauci

Why?

PROLOGUE

The Power of "Why?"

Why, Why, Why? Before I consider any material, design element, specialty finish or theme, I always, always, always ask myself, and my client, "Why?" Why are we doing this? Why is this here? Why are we using this material over another? Is it cost? Is it something you saw somewhere and just want to have it? Why should we choose it? Will it have a reason to be there? Why does it make sense? Honest answers to these questions will give the design process a greater chance of success!

For example, I was called to do some work in a bathroom. My clients only wanted to remove the carpeting (great idea) and change the room color. They did not want to change anything else. The shower had white tile and a white plastic basin. The cabinet top was a man-made faux white marble and the cabinet was painted white. The room had contemporary architectural lines. They showed me a sample of Old World travertine tile they selected. "Why do you want Old World travertine in a modern bathroom?" I asked them.

"Because this is what is most popular and most available," they replied.

I knew instantly this combination of colors and materials was not going to work together. Here's why. Aside from the architectural style being totally incongruous with what they were asking for, none of the other features supported an old world material. Clearly there were already too many different materials in this room. Adding another type of material was NOT going to work well.

To further compound the challenge, my clients showed me a picture from a magazine of a *decorative finish* they wanted on the walls. The room in the picture was old world European but their bathroom was not. Their bathroom was a small room with limited wall space. It was not large enough for a special finish to be appreciated. I felt the additional cost of a special finish would be of no value. This is a situation where a carefully selected solid color would be more effective. So here is the solution I came up with. I searched as many tile suppliers as I could until I eventually found what I was looking for. Are you ready? I used plain white ceramic tile. It isn't *fancy,* it isn't *right now,* but it works. It complements and is in context with all the other materials. It belonged there. Had I used anything else the first question most people would have asked would have been: "Why is that in here?" The Old World tile would have FELT out of place. For the walls I chose a very earthy yet energetic green. This gave the room a new personality and established harmony. They loved it! By staying in context with your architecture and other materials, you are more likely to create an environment that is pleasing and stylish.

Let me give you one more example of finding solutions by asking "Why?" and how doing so can save your project. I had a project where we were changing a modern home into a European style. In the kitchen the cabinets had flat slab doors and no exposed frames. The cabinets were separated by drywall approximately 4 inches wide. I realized if we applied fluted molding and corbels onto the drywall, installed face frames, new doors and crown molding, we could transform these modern cabinets into individual pieces of furniture.

Before

My design allowed us to minimize demolition by utilizing some of the existing framework. My clients loved the idea. They also loved the fact this would provide them a substantial savings. That's always good news. My client presented me with picture of the cabinet style they liked. We met with the cabinet contractor to sort out the details. I was then away from the project for a couple weeks while the cabinets were being fabricated.

When I returned, one of the cabinet pieces had some tumbled travertine stone samples leaning on the back wall. This piece had two upper cabinets on each end with an arch separating them, a lower wood counter and full lower cabinets spanning the base. The center was open as a flat screen TV was to be installed. I asked my client what the stone was for. She told me the cabinetmaker was going to use them for a backsplash. So what was my first question? "Why? A backsplash for what!? This is to be a piece of furniture."

I quickly explained the stone was not going work with the design and that we needed to use bead board. Why? Because bead board best represents the design we were building. Again, these cabinets were to appear as individual pieces of furniture. Why did this happen? The contractor along with the client, were following what many people do in a kitchen. In a typical kitchen the counter is commonly finished off at the back wall with a backsplash. Only this isn't going to be a typical kitchen. We are creating a personalized kitchen. Typical or common thinking does not apply. Additionally, this cabinet section was far away from any water source which automatically eliminates the need for a backsplash. They did not stop to ask, "Why are we doing this?" They certainly never asked, "What would be authentic in this situation?" I have never seen a piece of furniture with three and a half by three and a half inch travertine stone tiles on the back panel. Besides, even if we were going to use a backsplash, this stone would not have been appropriate. I have seen hand painted decorative tiles, but neither was going to work with this design. The moral of the story is the following: Before you do anything...ask yourself, your designer and your contractor...Why?

BEFORE

AFTER

Dino along with his brother Michael helping their parents paint the family home.

"We go through our everyday lives interacting with color. Everything we see is color with thousands of subtleties. A single color can represent a number of different shades. Thankfully we are in a world surrounded by color."

– Dino Fauci

1

COLOR

What Is Color?

"Color is subjective, personal, magical, inspirational, controversial and most importantly – color is ALIVE! It speaks its own language. The trick is knowing how to listen." -Dino Fauci

Listen to color? Seems like a silly statement, but is it really? There are many adjectives to describe color. I put them into two categories: technical (tone) and emotional (hue). *Tone* in simple terms is used to describe the *tint* or *shade* of a color (dark, light or deep colors). *Hue* is the value of colors within a color (a greenish blue for example). While both categories are present in every color, it's the emotional category that speaks with other colors. In the emotional category a single color can be described as having energy, being bright, clean, saturated or earthy, while others can be lifeless, dull or dead. Single colors can invoke a *feeling* but it's not until they are placed next to other colors that they begin to speak. Your eyes are your ears when using color. Color combinations will create either harmony, or noise (chatter). Harmony is when it feels good. Noise is when it doesn't. What makes this happen? Within a particular color are a number of other colors that make up the single color (hue). What you are listening to is how all the colors within a color relate to the different colors they are paired with. Confused? Have you looked at a color, yellow for example, and noticed it may look slightly red, too green or muddy? This is why the *perfect* yellow that you absolutely loved at the paint store doesn't look good in your space. The color yellow typically is not the problem. The colors that make up that yellow are causing the problem. They are not working in harmony with the surrounding colors. Many people will give up on a color because they don't realize this. It's not necessarily the color, but the *hue* of the color.

Let's take a moment to go over the basic *theory* of color. We can look at a color wheel and quickly gain basic understanding of complementary color relationships.

In color, complement means opposite. We can see how red is the complementary color to green. Yellow complements purple. Orange is the complement to blue. So what does this mean? In basic color mixing terms, if you have a color that seems a little too red, by adding green, the red will be less dominant. The same works if the color is too green, red will lessen the amount of green. This is true of all complementary colors.

We can also see on the color wheel how purple is secondary to red and blue. In other words, the mixture of red and blue make purple. Similarly orange is secondary to red and yellow. It seems basic, but red and yellow when mixed, make orange, therefore orange is secondary to the two primary colors which make it up.

The primary colors are red, yellow and blue. No mixture of any other colors can make the three primary colors. That is why they are called primary colors. Green, purple and orange, the secondary colors, come from combinations of two primary colors. There are also warm and cool colors. Red, yellow and orange are warm colors. They feel warm when you look at them. They are the color of warm things like fire, lava, and the sun. Blue and green are cool colors. They are the color of cool things like water and trees. Purple can go either way depending upon whether it has more cool blue or more, warm red. There are volumes written on color theory which will provide in-depth descriptions including the use of warm and cool colors. If you are not familiar with basic color theory, I suggest gaining a rudimentary understanding. A book that I found helpful is "Color in Interior Design" by John Pile.

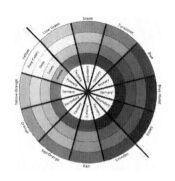

So rather than provide you with a lot of theory and color combinations that I know work well together, I feel it's more important to provide you with methods that will allow you to discover color combinations that will work best in your space. A list of colors, latest trends, or color of the year is of little to no use if they will not work in your space. My aim is to teach you how to *feel* color so you can understand it on a much deeper level.

So far you have learned that your eyes are your ears when working with colors. Color is first seen, and then felt. When you look at a color, what do you see? What do you feel? Do you get a feeling from it or nothing at all? Do you see a single color, or can you see a medley of colors? Do you see a preconceived idea of what that color is *supposed* to look like? This is often the name of the color. Many people get caught up on the name of the color and make a judgment based purely on its name, failing to really see the true color. They can't get past the name. I recommend not paying attention to the color name. It's only real use is to communicate the color with the paint store or with friends and family whom just love the color.

Let's do a little exercise that may help you understand how to see color. I will use brown for an example. What color(s) do you see in brown? Many people will describe the color only by its *tone* calling it either light brown, medium brown or dark brown. While they may be right, a color's lightness or darkness or *tone* is only one characteristic of a color. Can you describe the color by the hue? Which again are the colors that make up the brown.

Now study the color brown and look for other colors such as green and orange. Try to see as many colors within the brown as you can. Bring the object into different lighting conditions, perhaps in front of a window using natural light, to a darker room using artificial light, or even take it outside. Watch what happens. Do you now see colors you did not see before? Do you see other hues go away? Place it next to different objects. Now can you see the subtleties of colors within the color and how it relates to other colors? In order to choose the right color, it is necessary to see the various hues and to what degree they exist in the color you are viewing. This is true of every color.

When choosing a color it's imperative to go through this process. Don't worry, the more you practice, the quicker you'll be able to determine the hue and subtleties. The elements of each color should work with all the other pieces in the room. Therefore, if you are looking for a yellow, chances are, there are a few of the yellows which will work in your space. The correct yellow, or whatever color you are going for, will bring everything together in harmony and that is the objective.

THE PAINT STORE (DEPARTMENT)
COLOR DISPLAY CASE

"That overwhelming oversized display case with bright lights towering over you; there seems to be thousands of colors to choose from. You can almost hear the sounds of laughter as you approach as if it were saying to you, "There's no way you will get out of here with your sanity...go ahead...try!"

How many times have you gone into a paint store or the paint department at your local home improvement store, walked up to the display rack and started to feel your blood pressure increase? Confusion sets in and your head starts to spin. You came with a single color in mind but there are hundreds of variations of the color you thought you wanted. What now? Your next impulse may be to turn around and go cool out in the plumbing department before you run out of the store! Invariably you end up with a pocket full of colors you think *might* work. Of course if you have a significant other you will need to take the chips home so they can weigh in on it and hopefully they will not confuse you even further. The entire ordeal is confusing, frustrating, and fear of making the wrong choice is overwhelming. After you succumb to your confusion and lack of confidence, you do the only logical thing. You settle with the only logical solution.... white! Yes, that's it! White goes with everything. "Can't go wrong with white," you figure and off to the paint store again you go. If you are feeling really brave you may get some shade of off-white or cream. Do you know that white has more hues than any other color? I can mix up a match for any color you put in front of me, but white is the most challenging to match. White is sometimes a great choice, but we are going to step outside our comfort zone and pick some colors!

So, how do you make the right choice? What's the best method for narrowing down the options? It doesn't matter what color you think you want, as soon as you start looking, the choices appear to be endless. It seems like there are always too many choices…or are there? Although there may be hundreds of each color, only a few of these colors will be suitable in your space. How could this be you may ask? Isn't it just a matter of preference? Yes, but it's the space that has the preference. You may start with a particular color in mind, but you will learn the space actually has the final word. That is if you're listening.

I have a proven method of choosing colors that will allow you to get the colors you desire for your space. There really is a perfect color, or range of perfect colors, for your specific conditions (i.e. lighting, surfaces, décor, etc.). If you have never picked colors before, or have done so with little luck, relax. I will explain how this process is simple, fun and very rewarding. Once you understand how to choose colors you are going to gain more confidence for other design choices

Your color selection should enhance, support and create harmony with all of your art pieces, collectables and furnishings. When choosing a color, your goal should be to establish harmony with everything in the space.

Having the wrong color is like a flat note in a melody. It disrupts the entire song. Harmony in color is like harmony in music. When it is right, you don't even notice it. The music simply flows with all the notes working together as one piece of music. It merely feels right.

I am using music because I believe it's the perfect analogy. If you do not have a basic understanding of music theory, bear with me, hopefully you will still understand my point. When writing a piece of music, the key signature determines the notes that can be played. For example, the key of C major has no sharp or flat notes. Looking at the keys on a piano, if you are to play a major scale in the key of C, you would play only the white keys. If the scale is to be played in G major, there would be only one black key in the G scale, which is F sharp (F#).

Picture your furniture, flooring, art pieces and other furnishings as music notes. Think of the color of your room as the key signature. When writing music, the key signature is chosen first so you know which notes can be played. When choosing a color for a room that is fully furnished, you are actually working backwards.

Your goal is to find a key signature (color) that will support the notes being played (your furnishings and surfaces). Obviously you have more latitude with color than music, but approaching your color design in this way will help you visualize the final composition. As Mozart heard his symphony and wrote it down perfectly the first time, so too will it be for you to see your color design perfectly as you choose the colors. OK, maybe be not right away, but I'm an optimist. You are going to learn how to find that ONE color which will support everything else in the room. The colors you choose will create a feeling of support and harmony. You are going to become, like me, a *color composer,* even if you do not realize it.

Discovering how to do this is what this section is about. The following information will help you shed your fear of the dreaded color display case. You will chose colors with confidence. I will explain how the process of elimination works, how to see the many colors within a color, the effects of lighting on color, and define the anchor color. We will go over how to determine a particular tone, and which sheen level to use. Having a good understanding of these fundamentals will free you from the fear factor when choosing and using colors. It's not complicated. You can learn it. It is just a matter of learning how to LISTEN to color.

WHY LIGHTING IS SO IMPORTANT

I see many people make the mistake of thinking that if a room is 'dark,' they need to use a *light* color to make the room lighter. I completely disagree. If the room is dark, it will always be dark unless you change the lighting.

Here's a great illustration of lighting's effect on color. When I first learned to scuba dive, we brought an empty soda can with us to see the effects of atmospheric pressure. As we dove deeper and deeper, the can began to compress. Something else very interesting was also happening. The deeper we dove, the more brown the bright red can became. Why? Less light! No light, no color. As I continued to dive, I also noticed what appeared to be a dark brown sea fan, but once I shined my light on it, it was red, purple, orange or sometimes yellow. A brown star fish in my light was bright orange; a brown sea slug was green. Color which looks a certain way in one lighting condition, will definitely look different in another lighting condition. This is a basic concept, but is frequently overlooked.

This leads us to the following question: Why select color in a store under lighting which has nothing to do with the lighting in your space? Asking a sales person about colors for your space makes no sense. I have witnessed a sales person suggest a color for a customer based on the color's popularity! The customer explained that she is looking for a nice green color. She asked the sales person which green is currently popular? I watched this in total disbelief. I couldn't believe the customer bought the paint. It took everything in my power to not speak up. The colors you select must be taken home or to the location where they will be applied. Pick plenty of colors in the range you like and review those colors in all lighting conditions to fully understand how they will look in your space.

HOW TO MAKE THE
CORRECT COLOR SELECTION

Have you ever started to make a decision on a feeling then let your head get in the way? This holds true for color. If it feels right, most likely it is right. If you can't feel it, keep working on it and it will come. YOU CAN DO THIS!!!

Knowledge of some basic techniques will help eliminate the fear and get you to a place where you can choose the right color every time. As I explained previously, the perfect color picks itself. My job as a color consultant is not to pick colors. I listen to colors. The perfect color will speak up as the best choice. When choosing a color, listen to the color though your eyes. Look, Listen and Feel.

Listen to color? You may have noticed that I have mentioned this phrase a number of times so far. This is a term I came up with years ago. In fact, I have never heard anyone else use it so I have claimed it as my own. My motto is: "Color speaks." The trick is learning how to listen. When colors are put next to other colors, there is a vibration. It is either consonant (resolved), or dissonant (unresolved). Being able to see this vibration between colors is actually the ability to listen to color. When we listen to music, we hear it first and then it creates a feeling within us. When the music is consonant, we generally get a peaceful easy feeling. When it's dissonant (think of the music in the movie Jaws which is a minor 2nd) it creates tension. The relationship of colors is much like the relationship of music notes.

When you look at color relationships, start to notice how it makes you feel. When you approach color selection in this way, you will begin to see and feel color in a way you have never before. Gaining this skill will create a pathway to confidence and allow you to masterfully use color in a variety of ways.

Many clients say the same thing after I choose a color for them; "I would have never picked that color on my own!" Why? Mostly, it's because they have not learned how to listen to color. Other reasons can be fear of using color, or preconceived ideas of the use of color. Fear will stop you in your tracks and misguide you… release any fear you have and replace it with confidence.

Quite often when I am hired for a color consultation, the clients have already been to the paint store to gather color swatches they like. While this is helpful for me to understand which color family sparks their interest, most times the specific chosen colors are not going to work. That's usually the reason I get the phone call. So why does this happen? They like the colors, why won't they work? It's usually a number of reasons. Most likely because they picked the colors in the store where the lighting is completely different. As a result the color will look totally different in their space. Maybe they picked a color from something seen in a magazine or saw a color in a friend's home. They might have tried to match a color in one of their fabrics, or perhaps the color was a salesperson's suggestion. These are all common scenarios that most times lead to colors that are wrong for their space. Learning how to listen to color and also feeling the color are the first steps in color selection.

There is a very simple and inexpensive tool to help you start the color selection process. Almost all paint manufacturers sell what is called a COLOR FAN DECK. Color decks are traditionally a stack of every color that each manufacturer makes which spreads out like a fan (i.e. color fan or fan deck). The individual pages will typically start with the color in its darkest shade, and then gradates to the lightest shade by adding white. Paint companies' color decks may be organized differently but will most likely follow similar arrangements and also be grouped by hue. This means if you are looking for a red color, the orange-reds will be together, the blue-reds together, etc. Many decks are systemized by saturation such as neutrals, whites, pastels, mid tones and deep tones. Some will have categories titled classic, traditional and historic colors. These groupings may help you understand which color family will work best for your design.

Having a full line of colors in your space with the correct lighting is PRICELESS! I have found that most people either do not know these color decks are available to the general public, don't think to purchase one, or believe they are saving money by only taking home a few free chips. If you have to return to the store even once for more color chips, you are wasting more time and money. The color deck is the solution. This deck allows you to search through every possible color and combination each paint company has to offer.

Color fan decks range in price but are DEFINITELY worth the investment. Many home improvement stores may not sell color fan decks. You can almost always purchase them from major paint stores. I recommend calling in advance to check availability.

Once you have your fan deck, pick as many colors in the range you desire. Choosing colors from a small chip is challenging, even for a professional. I highly recommend taking the deck back to the store and ask for the larger chip samples (color cards) for each color. I also suggest getting a few additional color chips for each color choice. This will provide more options later and you certainly don't want waste time and money returning to the store for more color chips. The more choices you have on hand the better. I will explain more about this in the following sections.

COLOR TIP: I have had clients ask me to match the wall color to drapes, carpeting or a duvet. I resist. I always recommend choosing a color that COMPLEMENTS these larger materials rather than trying to MATCH the fabric. Save this color matching technique for smaller items like pillows and other accent pieces.

WHERE TO BEGIN?

Defining the Anchor Color

Where do I start?" is a question I get asked quite often. If your intention is to paint your entire house, I suggest starting with the largest "main room" which can be seen from other rooms. Starting this way will give you what is known as an "anchor" color. The anchor color sets the tone for the additional colors. If you plan on painting different colors in other rooms and they are all visible from the main area, it is imperative to make sure they are in harmony with the anchor color. Many make the mistake of picking colors for each separate room with no thought given as to how each color will work with the next. This needs to be a composition. You are composing a melody with colors rather than notes. If your space does not have such a room, I recommend starting with your most important room, the master bedroom for example.

Some of you may have children that are insistent that their bedroom be painted lime green or screaming pink. As long as they are not visible from the main areas, this will not have any effect on your space. If they are able to be seen from the main living space, search through the fan deck for a complementary color. There are ways to satisfy your children's desires for fun colors, and still have them flow with your décor. Don't be afraid to have every room a different color. I like to have as many colors as there are rooms providing the architecture will allow for this. The trick to achieving this is by establishing a harmonious relationship between the different colors, the anchor color and your décor.

USING THE COLOR CARDS

Most of the major paint stores carry index card sizes of each color that are found in the color fan deck. These are an extremely valuable tool that will aid you during your selection process. Once you have decided on your color choices from the fan deck, these index cards provide a greater understanding of your color composition.

This as I mentioned will most likely require a trip back to the store. Again, while you are there, be sure to select a few extra colors in the same range as your favorite color. This includes colors both in slightly different tones and different hues. Having a wider variety will give you more choices, and will also demonstrate the subtle differences between colors in the same or similar range. This process will help confirm your favorite choice is the best choice.

Once you have established the anchor color, go to the next room. Select the color you believe to be best for that room. If these rooms can be seen from one another, hold that color card up to the anchor color card and see if there is *harmony* between the two. If not, you will know it. It will be like a flat note. It just will not feel right. Try searching for another color in the same range but with a slightly different hue. The natural flow of color is extremely important.

If you are only changing one or two rooms, make sure the new color is harmonious with the existing colors. This can also be accomplished using color cards. To get an idea how well the new color will work with the other rooms, place the card with the new color on top or on the side of the door frame leading into the rooms you are NOT changing. Now stand back. Look at the relationship of the color card with the room color. This will give a very good idea of how the colors resonate. Repeat the process with each color you are planning to use. Do this against all other rooms you are not changing if they are viewable from each other.

THE PROCESS OF ELIMINATION

The elimination process is the best way to determine your best selection. Start by viewing your first choice. I start by holding the color card at arms length, closing one eye, and then slowly panning the room to see how it resonates with the lighting and décor. I also attach it to the wall with double-sided tape to allow me to view it from a distance. You may get an immediate feeling either way. Other times it may not happen right away. There are times when I am immediately 100% sure a color is perfect, but I will still place some of the other colors with varying hues and tones next to it just to be sure. This is the elimination process. By placing all your possible choices next to each other, and by using your new understanding of listening to color, you can now eliminate the ones that are not working. The best color choice will present itself. Do this with every color in every room.

Once you have gone through the elimination process, don't stop there. Take it one step further by making sure all the colors are harmonious while next to each other.

Start by placing all the color cards together like a deck of cards. Hold them at arms length to determine if they ALL complement each other. By placing all the color chips next to each other you will see and feel if there is harmony. If one or two colors feel like they are not working, you will need to decide if they will affect the space. Will they be isolated? If so you should be fine. If not, try finding a similar color with a slightly different hue. You will find that very small subtleties can make a BIG difference. I follow this process every time. And every time it has worked. When I put the cards together and it feels right, I can go to the paint store with 100% confidence I have made the right decision. Actually the space made the decision, I am just following direction.

This may seem like a lot of work but it's not. This process will not only train your eye to see color in a new way, it will also help your ability to listen to it. You will begin to notice how color makes you feel and gain the necessary confidence to choose colors that are best for your environment. Your space will guide you. Seriously!

CREATING THE SAMPLE

Once you have made your selection, and if you are still fearful of your decision, I strongly recommend purchasing a quart and painting the color directly on the wall or on a sample board. The sample board will obviously give you the ability to move it around the room. You can put the board behind or alongside important elements in the room. It is important, however, that the sample boards have the same texture as the wall surface in the room. For example, if your walls have an orange peel or knock down texture, purchase a can of texture and create sample boards to match your wall surface. The light will reflect the color differently on a textured surface than on a smooth surface.

One last suggestion when creating a sample: buy the SAME EXACT PAINT for your sample that you plan to use for the project. It is essential that the product you use on your samples is exactly the same quality and sheen you are using for the project. In other words, DO NOT purchase a cheaper product for the sample. It will not look the same.

If you are a perfectionist, as I am, you will want to note that a color mixed in a quart can be slightly different than one mixed in a gallon or five gallon container. Different quantities and qualities can produce slightly or even considerably different results. For the best results keep all variables the same including quantity. This isn't a major concern. I am only pointing it out. For the best results, purchase at least a quart of paint rather than the tiny samples that come in a pouch or 2 oz. cup.

SHEEN FACTOR

No Shine – Somewhat Shiny,
A Little Shiny or Very Shiny

When I ask clients which sheen they prefer, they tend to get a blank look on their face. Most people do not give this matter much thought. Typically they will reply with the question, "What choices do I have?" Or, "What do you recommend?" Some have it in their mind that they want something that is *scrubbable* because the children are always touching the walls. There is a sheen level for every situation and design requirement. In this section you will also discover why some sheen levels are better than others and I will clarify some common misunderstandings. For example, eggshell is actually a sheen quality and not a color (although some paint companies have eggshell as a color choice). Eggshell is between a flat finish and a satin finish.

As a rule, I am not a fan of sheen on walls. I design with the highest quality flat finish. Why? A high-quality flat finish gives the space a more distinctive feeling of depth and warmth. If a paint finish reflects too much light, it makes the room feel cold. Unless that is your intention, stay away from sheen. There are some environments, such as some modern interiors, where it can work. But primarily I only use a sheen level higher than flat for kitchens and bathrooms. Even in these areas I use the lowest sheen possible, i.e. the least shiny such as eggshell or satin. As long as the paint is classified as *scrubbable*, you will be able to clean the surface.

Those of you with children want to be able to clean the handprints easily so the logical choice would be a hard, shiny durable surface, i.e semi-gloss enamel. While this was true in the past, paint technology has advanced so you do not have to sacrifice a smart décor to have the ability to easily clean your walls. As I previously mentioned, many of the highest quality flat paints are very resistant and are *scrubbable*. If you desire a flat finish but are concerned about easy cleaning and durability, consult with your paint store or painting contractor as to which products will offer you the best of both worlds. Most quality manufacturers will have a product to satisfy your desires.

BATHROOMS

Choosing the Proper Finish

The paint of today has been dramatically changed to comply with new strict governmental and environmental regulations (this can vary by State). Paint companies have had to reformulate their product to reduce the Volatile Organic Compound (VOC) levels. These are considered toxic gases which are released while the paint dries. Why is this important? In order for paint companies to reduce VOC levels, they had to change the solvents and other ingredients they previously used. What they came up with for water-based paints is more soap. Soap has always been a solvent in water-based paints, only now there is much more. I stopped using oil-based paints over 20 years ago. Since then I have only used 100% acrylic water-based paints. I've been applying satin sheen, matte sheen and eggshell enamel in bathrooms with great success. I found the exterior grade works best because it was more durable against steam. With some of the lower quality water-based interior paints, an orange residue resembling rust forms on the walls and ceilings in areas which accumulated steam. However I do not have these problems with the highest interior or exterior grade paints. Many paint manufacturers have combined their formulas and rate the paint as both Interior/Exterior. Note: This orange residue is easily removed with warm soapy water and a sponge.

The reason I am bringing this subject up is because I recently used the most expensive line of paint from a manufacturer I have successfully used for years. Their new product line was known to be the very best on the market. This was to be the future of paint. As my clients requested, I used a matt finish in two bathrooms. A week later I got a call. There was a white film all over the walls and ceilings in both bathrooms! I had never experienced this before. I knew about the orange residue but never a white film. I'd never had a problem of any kind from top of the line paints.

I went to the paint retailer to investigate and this is when I learned the interesting fact that there are now even higher levels of soap being used as the primary solvent in the paint. This is done to eliminate the use of ethylene glycol. In order to resolve the problem I was instructed to wash the surface with warm water. After cleaning about four square feet of the surface, I rinsed my rag in the bucket and it quickly filled up with suds! The reason this happened is the matt finish remains slightly porous. When the bathroom became steamy the soap (solvent) in the paint had leeched out onto the surface creating the white film. How can you avoid this problem? I was informed to use at least a Semi-Gloss in areas which accumulate steam. Why? Semi-Gloss dries to a hard film which will prevent the soap from leeching out. Some companies are now making water- based paints with lower sheen levels specifically formulated to eliminate this problem. Ask your salesperson if they have water-based enamel specifically for bathrooms.

To my knowledge this is only true with water-based paints. I never had this problem with oil-based paints of the past. Since I no longer use oil paints I can not comment on the performance of today's new formulas.

WHAT TO DO NOW?

Once you have chosen your color or colors and are ready to paint, skip the following chapters and move into chapters 9 and 10 respectively. But if you'd like to learn some great techniques to add even more expression to your space, I suggest you read on about specialty finishes. Specialty finishes can add a completely new dynamic to your home or office.

Dino applying the final aging washes as the
scaffolding is being removed.

"Color is a very critical
thing. It's the emotional
part of a structure."

– John Hench

Faux Painted Yellow Sienna Marble

2

SPECIAL FINISHES

What is a Specialty Finish?

In the following section I will explain a variety of finishes that will encompass a large spectrum of faux and decorative finishes. These finishes have become very popular over the years. I will explain the difference between the two. In addition to these common techniques, you will also learn about finishes that are not so common such as character finishes, theme finishes and aging. You will learn how and why these finishes are used and often misused. Having a basic understanding of these specialty finishes will offer you infinite possibilities in creating your own personalized environment.

Specialty Finish is a very broad term. The term is used to describe a myriad of techniques. But in the simplest terms a specialty finish is anything beyond a base-coat. It is anything which exceeds what is generally considered traditional painting. These finishes require additional skills above and beyond the ability to apply basic traditional paint. Specialty finishes are a true art form.

WHAT IS FAUX?

"I remember as a kid, in my grandfather's workshop, seeing panels of various wood and marble. At the time I thought they were real. I didn't realize they were faux painted. Later my father told me how my grandfather would repair broken marble pillars in churches back in Italy and make walls look like wood panels. I had no idea back then in my grandfather's workshop that I would grow up using this inherited talent."

Faux, (pronounced "foe") is a French word meaning fake or false. Faux finishes have been used for years as a means to emulate rare and expensive materials. These finishes make it possible to save on construction costs. When it is too difficult, too expensive or too dangerous to install the real material, faux can provide an affordable solution. Other uses for these finishes are to repair and restore or add material that could not be duplicated.

All too often the term faux is misused to describe a decorative finish. Most of the time, it's really not a faux finish at all. A faux finish is one that authentically duplicates a natural surface such as stone, marble, wood, metal, concrete, fabric, paper etc. Sponging a wall is not a faux finish unless you use the sponge to create a natural surface. A sponged wall typically falls under the decorative finish category. Learning to differentiate between these different categories of specialty finishes will elevate you to a level of knowledge that goes beyond even some professionals who deem themselves *faux artists*.

Faux has both unlimited and limited possibilities. It's unlimited because faux finishes can solve design challenges, improve limited material selections, reduce cost and be used to repair damaged materials. Any surface that can be painted can be faux painted to resemble almost any material you can fathom. Previously painted wood, stones, bricks or concrete can be faux painted to look like the original material. Faux finishes also provide the ability to produce otherwise expensive materials and the ability to install them in difficult areas. This makes them a valuable design solution.

For example, I once repaired dark green marble walls in elevator lobbies of a high-rise building in Hollywood. Originally the building had to install emergency exit signage directly over the elevator call buttons. This meant drilling large holes the size of quarters into the marble to attach the signs. They were now being removed, leaving behind giant unsightly holes. My job was to patch and faux paint these holes to match the marble exactly. This was not such an easy task. The trick was to mix all the various colors to match the marble exactly, while developing the proper sequence of layers to disguise the repair. The repairs were invisible, so the job was a success. This saved the building owners thousands of dollars in replacement cost.

I have many times faux painted brick fireplaces that had been painted solid, back to their original condition. No one ever thinks the bricks are not authentic. I have a client in Newport Beach that has real brick flooring in her kitchen. Some of the bricks were damaged and needed replacing. She searched for months unsuccessfully looking for a match. I was meeting her to look at some other work in the home when she told me the story. I told her it wouldn't be a problem. I would make the bricks out of concrete and faux paint them to match. She couldn't believe it. Nor can anyone else. They were a perfect match.

As I mentioned at the beginning of this section, faux finishes have limitations. They are often used in places where the material would never be a serious design choice; like nine foot solid marble walls in a production home for example. Faux finishes need to be selectively chosen and convincing in areas of application. I have projects where I utilize faux finishes for decorative purposes too. For example, leather walls in offices and libraries, wood paneling and wainscoting are a common request I get. But I believe faux finishes are most effective when applied to smaller surfaces such as furniture, moldings, a table top, an inlay, wainscot, or accent pieces. Larger surfaces that would typically be made from natural material such as floors are great areas to apply a faux finish. When you are considering a faux finish, focus on being realistic.

I once marbleized an entire bathroom at my client's request. He chose a beautiful yellow sienna marble. He wanted it everywhere. This included the walls, ceiling, floors and even the doors. To make it look as authentic as possible, I panelized the stone by faux painting the joints just how it would realistically be installed. The finish was almost 100% believable. Why almost? Did you notice anything wrong with all the surfaces I marbleized in the bathroom? I tried to persuade my client, but it wasn't going to happen. Got it yet? The doors! I've never seen doors made from marble. Can you imagine how heavy they would be? My preference was to use a material for the doors which would have been more realistic. This also would have given the marble more value. Marble on the ceiling was a stretch but is sometimes done. The story was almost believable until the viewer looked at the doors. Something about that is unbelievable. The word *faux* is often misused, as are many faux finishes. Be selective where to apply these finishes. If misused, their value quickly diminishes.

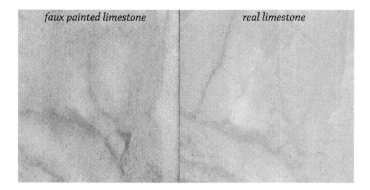

faux painted limestone   *real limestone*

FAUX TIPS: Faux finishes require years of practice to truly be authentic, but do not let this stop you from trying. Faux is a skill which can be learned. Start with something small and have fun.

The four key points when creating faux finishes are:

- diligence with color accuracy
- making sure you soften your work so even though you used a sponge to apply the paint, there is no evidence that a sponge was used
- use in realistic locations
- layering with multiple thin coats builds depth.

Layer, layer, layer! Assuming you have your colors right, multiple thin layers give your finish life and authenticity. Even if the color is perfect, without layers your work will look flat. The trick is lost without layers and your finish will fool no one. By the same token, even if your colors are slightly off, if you apply several layers your finish can turn out lively and authentic looking. This can be fun and extremely rewarding with a little concentrated effort.

WHAT IS A DECORATIVE FINISH?

A decorative finish is used to do exactly what the name describes...it decorates a surface. Sponging, ragging, color washing, strie, combing, trompe l'oeil, stenciling

and striping are considered decorative finishes. These finishes are very often referred to as faux finishes when in fact there is nothing faux or false about them. Most wall and furniture treatments you see are decorative finishes. They do not emulate any real material. They are not meant to look like wood grain, marble or stone. They are not intended to, nor do they replicate anything authentic. They are simply decorative and are therefore classified as decorative finishes.

Decorative finishes are often overused and more often than not, applied with a heavy hand. It seems almost everywhere you go, someone has smeared paint all over the walls. Now I'm not trying to give you the wrong idea, this is what I do. I love nothing more than beautifully finished walls. I just prefer subtlety over a finish demanding my attention for one reason or another. It could be a beautiful finish, but if that's all I notice, it's wrong for the space. The majority of decorative finishes I see are not decorative. They are visually demanding. In my opinion, they are the exact opposite of what they are intended to provide.

Like a wisely chosen color which supports, complements, and creates harmony in a space, a decorative finish should do the same. As I explained in the color section, you do not want the color to be a distraction. A decorative finish is secondary to the color but still needs to be in the same color family. Every additional color and technique used in a decorative finish has to receive the same amount of care and attention as the original color. Far too often I see a finish applied with no consideration to the overall effect. It really is unfortunate. The only thing in the room that people notice is the finish. This is definitely something I prefer to avoid.

Another obvious indicator of an ineffective decorative finish is being able to see how the finish was applied. A perfect example of this is seeing the starting and stopping throughout the finish. "What are those lines for?" I ask myself. When I look at a finish, I'm really not interested in how it was applied.

No evidence of the application method should be visible. When a finish is applied correctly, the viewer should be able to appreciate the results and not be distracted by the mechanics of the application. When I see the markings of a sea sponge all over the wall, I am fixated on the fact that someone smashed paint onto the wall with a sponge. When the paint or glaze is missing from the corners leaving a one inch frame around the wall, I'm left wondering if that was the artist's intention. Maybe they wanted to frame their masterpiece? When I see blobs of paint in the corners, I'm concerned that maybe the artist didn't see that. Are they coming back to fix it? When I see a finish where the artist used a big brush to smear glaze all over the wall to make it look aged, I'm left wondering, what is that supposed to be? Some people classify this as an antique or aged finish. Really? I have never seen anything age in that way.

The above examples describe the problem with a lot of the finishes I have seen. Most of these finishes people paid good money to have done. Any time either you or your specialty finish artist applies a decorative finish, pay close attention to these details. The details are what make your finish something special and truly decorative. If you do not have the ability to apply the finish yourself or the means to have a professional finish for you, staying with a carefully chosen color is best. I have seen many situations in which a simple single color would have been significantly better than a poorly chosen, poorly applied decorative finish.

So, how do you achieve professional results when you have zero experience? I will provide some very important tips and techniques so you can apply your decorative finish like a pro.

Tip #1: PRACTICE

Corners

"Applying a finish to a large flat surface is the easiest area to master. It's how you finish the corners that separate the professionals from the amateurs!"

If you want to practice and you are not willing to work on your walls, I recommend placing two sample boards together to create a corner. Most sample boards have no corners and are deceiving. When a faux/decorative artist shows you a sample board, ask to see pictures of this finish where you can see their corners. Corners separate the amateurs from the professional artists. As I explained above, bad corner work will destroy your job. Would you wear a shirt that did not have all the edges properly hemmed? So why would you accept a finish that is not properly installed, whether you did it yourself or paid someone to do it? My father once told me, *"You can do the best paint job in the world, but if there is one spot of paint on the floor, the job is ruined."* This is how I feel about poorly finished corners.

The best way to have successful corners is to mask the opposite side, leaving 1/16th to 1/8th of the opposite side wall exposed. This will allow some paint to find its way onto the other wall. This way, when you finish the other side, you can match up the design if need be.

Tip #2: START OFF SOFTLY & CREATE BALANCE

Much like layering a faux finish, starting softly with a decorative finish is a good practice. If you begin by applying the finish too heavily, you almost always have to start over. Remember, YOU CAN ALWAYS ADD, BUT IT IS VERY DIFFICULT TO TAKE AWAY.

Have you ever walked into a room and the only thing you notice is the paint finish? It is screaming for attention. It feels like nothing else in the room matters. It's like the 2000 lb. white elephant standing in the corner. You never want to let any single feature overpower everything else in the room. It will destroy your design. By beginning your finish with a soft hand, you can build it up slowly. This may seem like it takes more time, but trust me, it's better to *walk up* to your finish slowly than having to repaint the walls because you went too fast and too heavy. Learn to be patient. It will pay dividends later.

Be sure to focus on balance between the base color and the other colors you are using. I have seen many finishes where the colors are too contrasting and too bold. This will make your finish look amateurish. You will achieve a much better finish by applying a few less contrasting colors over each other than by using two strong contrasting colors. Again, you can always add bolder colors later.

Balance your colors as well as your technique. Balance the technique? What does that mean? If every time you apply the glaze or paint with the same amount of pressure, same direction, same consistency, same movement, you will get the rubber stamp effect. By balancing your application technique, you will create variety thus minimizing the evidence of how the finish was applied.

"What you think about, you bring about." This is such a true statement when applying a decorative finish. I was on one of my first decorative finish projects while for working for Melody Scott. I found myself getting lost in thought. I went into auto-pilot. When I stepped back to look at my work, I could see a section of the wall that looked different. That was the auto-pilot section. I had to fix that area. That was a big lesson for me. Thoughts and feelings come out through our hands. It's important to stay focused. Otherwise you're likely to have rubber stamps and auto-pilot marks all over your walls.

Tip #3: HAVE A REASON TO BE THERE

"It is great to have a focal point, but unless you are creating a theme finish and are using that finish to tell a story, I feel the focal point should never be the finish."

Relevance is very important in designing a space. Picture an elegant modern home with sleek furnishings, exquisite art pieces and…an 18th century Italian coffee table complete with gold leafing. What is the antique table doing here!? The Italian gold leaf table has now unfortunately become the focal point because it is out of place. It may be a beautiful table but it certainly doesn't belong in this space. While this is an obvious example, I have seen this mistake in the form of paint finishes. There seems to be a misconception that wall finishes need to be strong. I find this to be not true.

When you are choosing a finish for your space, it's important to make sure it has a reason to be there. Will it add support to the other elements or be a distraction? Often my clients will show me magazine clippings of finishes they like. While these finishes may suit the space in that photograph, the finish may not have a relationship with their space. I prefer to guide my clients towards a finish that will complement their environment or to single colors that will add value to the space. The real question here is, "Will what you want add value?" Many times just the right color might be enough.

During the past decade it seems decorative finishes have shown up everywhere and anywhere, and more often than not, without much consideration to the context in which they are being used. Applying a decorative finish without defining its reason and value to be there can be a big mistake. When a finish is applied without proper consideration and expert execution, it makes the space seem confusing and unbalanced. Ask yourself, "What is this supposed to be?"

For example, a color wash is generally used to make a surface appear well aged. A slight patina provides a sense of maturity. Multiple color washes using various colors can be used to create a colorful effect. But will it be appropriate for the space? Always remember to ask yourself, "Why?" Will it add to the decor? Will it support the design or will it stand alone? Once again, a decorative finish should always be just that, decorative. It should add value without being obnoxious.

DECORATIVE FINISHES WHICH WORK BEST!
Fabric Effect

I have had the best results with finishes such as *tone-on-tone* applications. I prefer this fabric finish because of the soft and warm appearance it provides.

For example, once I was asked by a client to match a piece of fabric that would be used in the master bedroom for accent pillows. This was a tone-on-tone fabric with a slight shimmer and soft floral pattern. I created this finish by matching the color to the fabric and then applied the base-coat in a flat sheen. I then used the same color but slightly lighter in a semi-gloss and used a rag to simulate and replicate the texture of the fabric. Before applying the ragging, I thinned the paint slightly so it would be slightly transparent. When viewing the finish straight on, you can barely see the finish (much like the fabric). But as soon as you view it from a slight angle, or in indirect light, the ragging texture is visible. It created a feeling of warmth in the room without controlling the space. This is an example of a soft but powerful effect. This finish adds value to the room without being overpowering.

Stripes

Stripes can add an element of sophistication and elegance. They can also be fun and playful. You can create a stripe combination to suit a variety of situations. It all depends on the color scheme and size of stripes

you choose. I have found tone-on-tone stripes are very effective. Much like the fabric finish described above, it is understated but adds an element of surprise. Because of the soft contrast, it is not really noticed as much as it is felt. This is my top priority when creating a finish. The viewer has to experience the feeling long before they realize what technique has been used, if ever!

I often use stripes with low to medium contrast. Strong contrasting stripes work best in areas which demand a bold statement. Bold stripes are also more playful. Powder rooms, for example, are great rooms to be bold in. It depends on your taste. I have also broken up a stripe with a pinstripe between the main two stripes. A color slightly darker than the other two colors works well. Even a metallic pinstripe works really well. It really is a great effect if the space will support it. Another finish which works well with stripes is *negative ragging* or *positive ragging* over the stripes. This works best on the less contrasting stripes. If you are looking for something with some shimmer to it, try using a satin or matt sheen base coat. Mask off the stripes and then use a very thin metallic or pearlescent glaze over the base coat. Once again, this finish is subtle but very effective because it adds just enough interest to the space while allowing room for other design elements.

Patina Effect

The term patina is quite often associated with the blue-green color that occurs on copper either naturally or artificially by the use of chemicals (acid). A patina is in fact, a superficial covering. This is a process that happens over time and can be aesthetically appealing. A patina can occur on a variety of surfaces; not only copper. It adds character, definition and historical elegance.

A soft patina finish has a much greater effect on a space than does a heavy color wash. Why? Think about a heavy color wash on an interior. How did it get like that? Why did it get like that? Would an interior of a home really become that aged? No, it would not! Many times I see a heavy color wash on walls and ceilings because the installer did not have the skills or vision to create a softer look. Frequently a finish is installed in one space for a particular design or theme and then duplicated in another room for no valid design reason.

Unless you are creating a theme of heavy aging, I recommend staying away from these finishes. I have found heavier patina effects work best on separate pieces such as furniture and accent pieces. These items can justify the story of being old whereas your walls are less convincing. Once again, an understated finish on walls and ceilings is much more esthetically appealing. It provides the viewer a true sense of a time period and matured elegance. Using a color just a few shades darker than the base-coat works best for this treatment.

THE EFFECTS OF AGING

The effects of time and environmental conditions have on materials are similar to the lines on our faces as we age. I understand that we live in a time when everyone wants to look and feel younger and that's fine. There is nothing wrong with looking our best. However the lines on our faces give us character. It's our story. While this may not matter to you personally, you may not want to dismiss the beauty of age in other areas. I have learned to appreciate the aging effect on everything...especially architecture. Clean and new is wonderful but it has no story. Aged architecture has a story. And it's that story which makes it interesting!

Aging is good. It creates character. If you have ever been to Europe or even seen pictures or movies of European architecture, you know how beautiful an aged building or surface can be. The character which has occurred on these surfaces over time is marvelous. Its appearance actually tells the story of its history. How disappointed would you be if you traveled to Venice, Italy, and all the buildings had been repaired and freshly painted? How would you feel if the canal walls had been scrubbed clean of moss? How about if you drove through the farmlands of the United States and all the old barns had no visible aging, but instead were coated with a fresh coat of paint? So much character would be lost. The historical story of those structures would be erased and criminally left untold.

There is so much beauty in something that has been aged. Have you ever noticed the various colors in the moss growing on a building or rock? How about the beautiful silver color from aged wood and all the subtleness of other colors of the wood? How about the gradation of colors in a deeply colored plaster wall?

Many people look at these as just being old or just see it as it is with no other thought or appreciation. I look at it as art. *Nature's art*. Time creates beauty. It's a joy to be able to see and appreciate it.

CHARACTER FINISHES

Character finishes are to a theme artist what words are to a writer. Techniques are your vocabulary. The larger your vocabulary (range of techniques), the more interesting the resulting story (the finished product) will be.

Character finishes tell a story with paint and other mediums. They are part faux finish and part character aging. In other words they are *fake-faux* finishes combined with other techniques meant to mimic or duplicate a particular substance. They are used to mimic the time or environmental aging process of that substance. Aging techniques tell a story.

Character painting gives us the ability to recreate the story of a time period using paint. These techniques originated in the motion picture industry and were later utilized and perfected by theme parks. When I say perfected, I am referring to the refinement of the techniques. Methods used to create finishes for the camera are much more exaggerated than ones used for the naked eye. In recent years, entertainment establishments such as Las Vegas hotels and casinos have utilized character aging and theme painting techniques. When done correctly they are truly amazing. When done incorrectly, the results can be disastrous. Let's look at the definition of the techniques and how they are used.

Character painting portrays the effects of weathering and aging while enhancing the architectural and historical character reflected in the design. Character or theme painting is the use of specific techniques which artificially recreate the look of any material and a particular time period.

Character and aging techniques can be considered a form of faux finishing. They represent the effects of time and exposure to the elements on finishes and substrates in the real world. When using these techniques, you are faux painting a natural condition. I prefer not to classify this as *aging* because without the previous explanation of the beauty of aging, most people almost immediately envision old and dirty when they hear the word. This is partly due to the fact that many painters / faux artists think by sanding off the finish in random locations and applying a dirty wash, they have created an aging finish. Without a story (how did it get that way?) most aging finishes you see are really decorative in nature because it's a fictional story. It's not how it really happened. Character finishes are a *true* story of how things could happen. This understanding is extremely valuable when you want to add some historical character to a structure. Even If you never attempt this finishing technique, hopefully you will now look at aging with new perspective and appreciation. I will paint you a picture… a mental picture.

Let's say you have a very old building that had been painted many times through the years. Suppose it has been neglected for the past 10 years. It is exposed to harsh conditions. The paint has oxidized and is peeling away exposing the plaster, bricks, wood, or other substrate underneath. Years of dirt and pollution have collected. There might be mold and moss growing in the damp shaded areas. The paint on the windows could be cracking and falling away. The wood trim may have turned gray and lost its color. A building in this state would be considered an eyesore to some. In the right setting, it's full of character. This character is the result of effects of environmental conditions. A painted surface which fakes the actual condition is left to interpretation. It is not actually duplicating a specific natural material. Character finishes can be considered environmental condition finishes.

Why is any of this important to you? It is important because these techniques can be utilized in your environment to create amazingly beautiful results.

Although these applications are most common in the theme park and entertainment industries, they are becoming increasingly popular in private homes, restaurants and retail markets. Some examples would be to add character to the exterior of structures and landscape items such as waterfalls and faux rocks around swimming pools and other water features.

If your property has a particular architectural design, applying a character age finish will dramatically enhance it. For example, if your home is Mediterranean style, most likely it will have a clay tile roof. Many of these tiles will accept aging washes. Why would you want to do that? Well, if you are going to apply some character to your house you will need to tell the complete story.

Applying light aging washes and even some green moss to the tiles will really enhance the character of your home. The aging washes will soften the *newness* of the tiles. As for the moss I'm not suggesting painting moss over the entire roof, only in a few selected areas that would naturally grow there over time. Moss works best in corners and shaded areas.

Now let's look at your trim. This includes your fascia boards, windows, shutters, garage doors, etc. Are these elements painted or stained? Regardless of their current finish you can add an element of time by slightly bleaching corners and areas that would be most affected by the sun. Then by applying a slightly darker color than the original base color as a patina wash. This will finish the job and make everything look awesome. Remember, the idea here is NOT to make it look damaged, but just to add some character.

The plaster will quite possibly be the most difficult surface on which to apply a finish due to the large surface area involved. I do not recommend applying this finish on a sand finish stucco surface. Why? The wash hangs onto the sand and creates *runs*. It can be done but it's very difficult to control and make look authentic. The plaster surface needs to be smooth or have a hand trowel cat-face finish. Plaster over time becomes very beautiful. It fades and becomes lighter in sunny dry areas and darker in shaded wet areas. The combination is very appealing. This allows you wide creative parameters. You can be as subtle or bold as you like, keeping in mind the storyline needs to stay in context with all of the other surfaces.

If attempting to apply a character finish to the plaster, there are a couple of manufacturers who make a lime base paint which will naturally age over time. These paints still require some skill to apply properly but are definitely much easier to install than a character painted finish. These paints are meant for plaster surfaces and work best on smooth or cat-face plaster and offer acceptable results. The problem I have with these paints is that they have more of a homogeneous appearance than a finish applied by an artist, and there is no controlling their aging effect. Even so, it's a good alternative.

The biggest issues I notice with most exteriors are finishes that are decorative rather than aged. A decorative finish does NOT tell a true  story of how a structure would have naturally aged. It leaves the viewer wondering, "What is that? Why does it look like that?" I have seen homes where the finisher applied a sponge finish or dark heavy washes in an effort to age the building. Unfortunately it looked more like paint was running down the wall rather than the intended aging effect. Another effect I often see poorly executed are "break-away" areas in the plaster, exposing bricks or other substrate underneath in far too many areas. This makes the overall effect unrealistic. It looks more like a structure at a miniature golf course. Most people would not want their home to look like an amusement park. When done correctly, an aged character finish will represent a time period thus creating an interesting visual STORY. You want the viewer to fully understand the story of the structure so that they can appreciate its beauty. You certainly do not want the viewer to look at your home and become disenchanted with the finish and have them ask, "Why is that there?" If your finish is not going to be authentic, I suggest spending your money elsewhere.

Prior to embarking on the process of applying a character finish, be sure the architecture of your home will support the design. Mediterranean, Spanish, Tudor, Cape Cod and other design specific structures lend themselves to character finishes. It would be very difficult to realistically age a typical production home that has no architectural identity.

UNDERSTANDING THE PROCESS

If you plan to apply a character finish on your own or plan to hire a theme painting company to do it for you, it will be helpful for you to understand the process of character painting. Character painting as well as character aging, involves applying multiple layers. The area must also be viewed and evaluated intermittently during the application process. Traditional painting is surface preparation, primer and finish coat application. Traditional painting is a linear procedure. Character painting/aging, is a development process which CANNOT be done in a predetermined number of steps. Although the basics can be established, multiple layers are required to achieve the overall final product.

Stepping back and viewing the area being worked on during the application process of each layer is imperative. Viewing your work from a distance is crucial for the proper adjustment of strength and color. Different lighting conditions are also important when evaluating the finish.

This means if your project requires scaffolding, the boards will need to be removed at scheduled intervals to view the work. This will add to the overall cost, but will be worth the money once the project is finished.

Character painting/aging is an art. The canvases just happen to be structures, i.e. walls, ceilings, floors. Artists of all mediums utilize distance to evaluate their work. Similarly, field work also requires distance. Try standing one meter from a painting and look at it. Then put a much larger distance between you and the painting and observe the difference. Now try looking at that same painting in different lighting. Do you notice the changes? Painting canvases is not much different from painting structures. The brush strokes are larger.

Some techniques are modified, but the requirements are the same. Light, distance, and the ability to view the work unobstructed, are all requisites for successful application of finishes. Having a good understanding of this will assist you in communicating with your contractor. It will also aid you in understanding what is required to achieve authentic results.

Creating, Restoring & Enhancing Natural & Manmade Surfaces

Architects, designers and builders have two options when choosing materials, 1) Real (live) or 2) Artificial (simulated). Artificial materials generally tend to appear unrealistic and sometimes plastic. They frequently lack enough variation in color and shape to be convincing. Many times the color selection is too limited for the design's intent.

Real stones or bricks may not be available in the right color or they may be cost prohibitive, I have seen some very believable products. However, I feel something is missing from some of the offerings. Real live materials have energy. That's what is missing with these synthetic materials. Energy! With just a little paint magic these materials can come to life.

In the case of a damaged surface (broken, graffiti, overspray, etc.), a satisfactory match for the existing material may not be available. An experienced finisher with character paint skills is capable of solving all these problems. Colors can be matched to existing surfaces or they can be made to just enhance a poor color palette.

Just a few colors added to a limited color palette will dramatically transform the overall appearance entirely.

One situation I run into often is bricks or stones which have been painted over. Most people first think of sand-blasting to return the material to its natural state. Another alternative is the use of toxic chemicals to strip paint off. Even with these techniques, getting paint off completely is nearly impossible. Damage to the substrate can also easily occur with use of such harsh methods.

Character/theme painting is the solution to all the surface problems just described. Previously painted surfaces can be painted to resemble their original condition. Natural or artificial surfaces may both be altered or completely changed. Virtually ANY surface can be altered, enhanced, restored or imitated with proper techniques, knowledge and materials. When applied and sealed correctly, these finishes will not only fool even the most discriminating eye, but will last many years.

"Painting is poetry that is seen rather than felt, poetry is painting that is felt rather than seen."

– Leonardo da Vinci

I believe painting is both seen and felt!

Dino and authentic sushi chef, Yasu-san at Sushi Laguna in Laguna Beach, CA Photo by Reiko Sugioka

Sensei Yasu-san observing my cutting technique.

3

ARCHITECTURAL STYLE

"You can't be something you are not!"

Have you ever been to a sushi restaurant where the chef behind the sushi bar is not from Japan or any other Asian country? Now there is nothing wrong with a non-Japanese person making sushi, however, it doesn't look or feel very authentic. We expect Japanese chefs to be making sushi at a Japanese restaurant. Why? Because making sushi is a Japanese cultural art form that takes years to master. Having anyone other than a skilled Japanese chef making your sushi could raise some concern due to the possibility of receiving less than an authentic sushi experience. I picked this analogy because sushi is so strongly associated with Japanese culture. I happen to know a few sushi chefs that are not

Japanese and they make incredible sushi. My point here is this: as good as these chefs are, the fact still remains they can't be something they're not. They'll never be Japanese. With Japanese sushi chefs I truly enjoy the experience. When I eat sushi, I like to feel as if I am in Japan for that moment. It provides me with an authentic experience. I want to believe it. Authenticity is equally important in architecture. A structure can't be something it's not.

Picture yourself walking into a 1950's style home where someone has attempted to transform it into a Mediterranean Villa. They may have used travertine flooring and old world décor, but is it truly a Mediterranean style? It is the same principle as the non-Japanese guy making your spicy tuna hand roll.

The only way in which this style combination could work, is if the structure is completely remodeled AND IF the architecture is authentic within that style. Unless you are planning to reshape the entire house, I always teach staying true to the original architecture of the home or building. This does not mean if you have a 1970's style home, you have to have avocado green shag carpeting and burnt orange walls, although that would be kind of cool. Getting caught up in the latest trends or a particular theme can be a mistake, especially if the trend is not in context with the architecture.

Accepting and appreciating something for what it is can be a liberating accomplishment. For example, I was recently working in a custom built 1960's California Ranch Style home which had not been remodeled. It was beautiful. The entrance still had the original terrazzo floors. How many homes still have authentic terrazzo floors? This floor really set the stage for the rest of the home. This home is very stylish, well kept and reflected the owner's lifestyle. Many may feel it would need to be updated and changed into something it was not. I loved it. It remained authentic to the architecture. I was asked to transform the kitchen, laundry room and the bathroom which was located just off the kitchen area.

I was only changing the walls, ceilings and trim. Everything else was staying. The kitchen walls had wall paper left on them from the 60's. It was authentic of that era, but certainly not a reason to keep it. It needed to be removed. Keeping within the style of the house and existing decor, I chose a yellow for the kitchen and laundry room which complemented the furnishings, building materials and the other viewable rooms. It also provided the space some fresh energy. A clean, very soft patina for the walls was the next step. I added just enough patina to represent a sense of time without looking dirty or out of place. I created the patina by toning the base color a few shades darker. Keep in mind the kitchen was not being remodeled so the cabinets, appliances and flooring remained. They were all in pristine condition with a sense of age. The patina helped create the story that the new color belonged there. Applying only a fresh coat of paint in my opinion would have looked out of place. It now has a relationship with the surrounding materials, thus keeping it authentic.

In the bathroom I selected dark blue and white stripes with a gold metallic pinstripe which separated the white and blue. This gave the small bathroom a more spacious feeling by making the walls seem taller.

It also added a level of sophistication which was in context with the rest of the home.

Prior to embarking upon redecorating your home, it is very important to understand your architecture. Unless you have a custom built home, many production homes do not have any particular style or at best, the style is "implied" as opposed to authentic. So what should you do? Look for architectural elements within the space that you can use in your design.

I have another story to help explain this. I was designing a color palette for a small space in Ventura, California which had an implied *loft* style. But it was truly just a box. The upstairs master bedroom had an opening into a small sitting area. On one side of the opening there was a piece of wall extending six inches from the left corner. The wall on the opposite side was about five feet wide. It felt out of balance and I wanted to separate the rooms.

To do this, I simply painted the six inch section a darker color and six inches of the opposite wall. This created a frame. It now appears as two columns which separate the two rooms. It created balance and separation in an unbalanced area. The open floor plan was perfect for using different colors in each room to provide each area with its own identity. The railing in the upstairs bedroom which looked over the living room below was originally painted a cool gray. To add warmth, I used a bronze metallic paint and applied highlights to the details adding authenticity to the finish making it look like polished bronze. Now what once seemed like an empty box, took on the feeling of a personalized home. It felt great even before the furniture was brought in. This is when you know you have created harmony.

I also designed finishes for a semi-custom home that had an implied Spanish architectural style. The long entry hall had a series of arches made from drywall. I used this architectural element to create a theme for the house. I faux painted the arches to be stacked travertine stone. This completely transformed the house and gave the arches an identity along with providing the image of structural support. This type of finish may be beyond your means or simply not your taste in which case using a single separate color would be enough to add interest and provide separation.

To expand on the theme, I used the dining room to create the look of an old historical Spanish mission. I painted the walls to resemble aged peeling paint with the plaster exposed. I faux painted the white plaster fireplace surround as limestone. I also wood grained the white baseboards to match the wood crown molding. I antiqued two built-in cabinets. It was beautiful with the faux travertine stone arches. This may seem a bit extreme but it all worked really well. Why? Because the finish and color palette are in context with the architecture. When you walked into this home, it had a story. And you believed it. My point with these two examples is to identify your architectural elements on which to build and establish your design direction.

To view more about the faux travertine arches and the rest of the interior I mention here please visit: dinofauci.com and go to the Testimonials page.

UNDERSTANDING YOUR ARCHITECTURE

Some homes have a very obvious style while others may leave you utterly confused. This was exactly the case in the home in which I grew up. It was a production home built in 1965 in a northern suburb of Los Angeles. These houses were basically boxes with a roof which was typical California 1960's through 1980's tract homes. The style of these homes was usually confusing and in my opinion absolutely horrible.

How does a house like this find an identity? The first step is to identify the architectural elements on which you can begin to build its identity. As I said before, styles are sometimes implied and not at all distinctly defined. An arch can lean towards Mediterranean or Spanish styles, but they can have straight lines and geometric shapes which are more modern or contemporary. The furnishings play a major role in defining the style of a home. Modern furniture in an old world European style home might not be the easiest combination, but it can be made to work. Similarly, if you have old world furniture or an eclectic collection with no particular style in a modern home, that can work too! Confused yet?

The trick here is COLOR. First, analyze your architecture, surface materials and other elements and define your style parameters. Look for details and shapes to work with. You are looking for something to build upon. Some of these items could be arches, moldings, ceiling shapes, doors, windows etc. There may not be anything special and that's ok. There are colors and finishes that can bring just about any mixture of styles together. As a suggestion, I would resist trying to force a style into a space just because you like that style. The key here is to take the time to work with colors, going through the elimination process. Starting with a complete understanding of your architectural style and considering how that style works with your furnishings and other surfaces in the home (flooring, counters, etc.) and then tying them all together with color, is critical to tackling the design challenge of personalizing your space.

UNDERSTANDING YOUR SURFACES

What are your surfaces? They are flooring, counter tops, doors, moldings, walls and ceiling textures. All play a significant role in how you should approach your design.

They will also give clues to what your particular style is. Remember, the purpose of this book is to help you transform your space only using color and finishes, so it is important to determine how to work with the existing surfaces.

Let's begin by talking about wall and ceiling texture. Other than a beautifully hand troweled plaster finish, why are walls and ceilings usually textured? One reason is to save on cost. A contractor can hide a lot of imperfections with a blown on orange peel or knockdown texture coat.

How about acoustical ceilings, otherwise known as *cottage cheese* ceilings? I never liked that material. I remember as a kid my dad would spray paint them white and then blow gold or silver glitter into the wet paint. He sometimes used blue or pink glitter in children's rooms. I am not sure where that style came from. I am happy it's gone. I have also seen a circle or starfish design on ceilings and walls in places like Florida and North Carolina. Depending upon where you live, you may have some odd textures to deal with.

Machine applied textures do not work well with specialty finishes. These areas will need to be skim-coated to a smooth finish. If you are going for an Old World look, a simulated European hand trowel finish works well. The point here is to identify your wall and ceiling surface and plan accordingly.

Your other hard surfaces should be considered as well when selecting color and design. It is important to work with what you have. Make choices that will bring it all together and create harmony and authenticity. Even if you cannot be specific with an overall definitive style, if you complement every surface in the space with the right color choices, you can create an illusion of authenticity. If it looks great, if it feels great, it is great!

*Distressed and aged wall unit adds
historical elegance to the room*

Dino painting faux travertine arches

European plaster on walls, mural on canvas painted by Danny Montes, and woodwork painted dark give the room European flair while staying in context with the architecture.

"Dino is an artist in the field of color and texture. We had hired another designer but she just couldn't understand our needs. He listened to our desires and feelings with patience. He understood the colors we liked and made them work. Our home now flows, shadows and inspires. Our desires have truly been met."

– John and Judy Wallace

4

UNDERSTANDING YOUR ENVIRONMENT

Lighting; Natural & Artificial

Early morning light is warm, afternoon is cool and evening is slightly warmer than morning.

To understand your environment is to recognize a number of aspects such as architectural style, furnishings, surfaces and most importantly, lighting. How light affects the room is extremely important. It will determine the effect on your paint as well as all the other elements of the room. The floor color, for example could reflect color onto the walls and ceiling. This would have to be a factor in color choice for that room.

Natural light is the most important and artificial light is secondary. Of course the importance of the light source depends upon the actual lighting in the room. If there is no natural light then artificial light becomes most important.

There are many artificial light choices, so changing your light bulb, could dramatically change your décor. As I explained in chapter one, choosing your colors in the exact lighting condition is critical. I had a customer who had chosen a marble which she thought was tan for her master bath along with a deep mahogany colored wood floor. The materials had already been installed when I arrived. Although the two materials looked good together, they were not chosen in the actual environment and without any consideration to the paint colors. As a result the tan marble had a pink hue (remember, brown is either red or green). I mentioned to my client, the marble was rather pink and it would be a challenge to choose a color which would work well with the marble and also complement the color in the master bedroom. My client looked confused when I said the stone was pink in hue. Once I started putting colors against the marble, she quickly saw the amount of pink in the stone. She really couldn't believe it.

This is a perfect example of why it is extremely important to choose colors and materials in the actual environment with the exact lighting conditions. This bathroom had a mixture of natural light and artificial light. Although the room received a good amount of natural light, artificial light was almost always present. Therefore, I chose the paint color in both lighting conditions. Remember, understanding the lighting in your environment is critical to choosing colors and finishes. I was able to find a color that complemented the room and worked well with the master bedroom color. I used a bold dark (red hue) brown on the Pullman (cabinet) which demanded some attention. This provided additional interest in the room so the wall color was now secondary. It worked.

FURNISHINGS

Your new colors and finishes will be the backdrop for your furnishings. Think of it this way: your furnishings and accessories are the picture, and your walls, ceiling and floor are the frame. When framing a picture you don't want either the picture or the frame to dominate or compete with each other. The goal is for the frame to complement the painting. The matting should soften the transition and help bring your eye to the focal point of the painting. This is harmony in design. Your eye is attracted to the focal point as it also appreciates all of the other features. When choosing a color, think in these terms and it will help you make sense of which direction you should go. It will also narrow your options which will make proper color selection far more manageable.

The style of furnishing can sometimes dictate the direction of color selection. Typically modern and contemporary furniture lend themselves to cleaner colors. Traditional large dark wood pieces (antiques) look better with warm earthy colors. Whites and neutrals can work with both. This is not a rule; only a generalization.

As I pointed out in chapter one, white goes with just about anything. I'm not saying don't use whites and neutrals. Sometimes they are the best choice. Many times you will be working with a neutral space in which case my ambition is to encourage you to add color and make a dramatic transformation. If the clean look of white is what you are after, by all means do it.

ROOM TYPE
Dark, Light, Big, Small

The type and size of the room are also factors which can play into your color selection. If a room is large with a lot of light, what should you do? Keep it light or try to make it appear smaller with a darker color? What about a small room that gets little to no natural lighting? Do you paint it white so it will feel larger? Is there a right answer to either room? No, not really. It's all a matter of preference. I do have my theory. Here it is. Play off the positives of the space as opposed to attempting to hide the perceived negatives. If there is an absolute negative, such as some unsightly feature, by all means disguise it. But, if it's only a perceived negative, focus on the positive instead.

There is the school of thought that if a room is large with a lot of light, you can use a darker color because it won't seem as large. I struggle with this theory because I would rather create the best environment by considering the reality of the space. If the room is big and bright, celebrate that. Focus on the spaciousness of the space and all of the positive attributes. Let it be big. Let it be bright because it is! If you definitely do not like the spaciousness of the room and your goal is to make it feel smaller, a really dark color or specialty finish may help to some degree. But I would also recommend diffusing the light source and also try adding larger or more furniture.

If the room is small and has little light, some believe using a light color or white will make the room feel larger. I also struggle with this theory. Why? Unless there are plans to make the room bigger and change the lighting, I like to let the room be what it is by selecting a color or finish which will add to the existing personality of the room. I prefer to use medium to dark tones. Painting a small room a light color will only emphasize the fact that it is a small room. Let the room be what it is and play off the positives.

I find small light painted rooms to be cold. If you have to be in a small poorly lit place, wouldn't you rather feel comfortable and cozy rather than cold and on edge? Picture yourself being in a small space where the walls and ceiling are cold and lifeless. It brings attention to how close everything is and amplifies the smallness of the space. In my mind it creates an image of an interrogation room rather than a great living space.

Now, picture the same room with the walls and ceiling in a warm color. This will create the feeling of having a blanket over your shoulders while reading a book. In this situation the small size of the space is not accentuated. Instead you are left with a calming feeling and no longer notice the size of the room. How the room feels is what stands out, not the size.

Understanding the size and light source of your environment is essential to creating a space which looks great and feels even better. When you walk into a room and your first sensation is a feeling, you know it is a great environment. If you walk in and your eyes are moving around the room darting from one element to another, something is not working. The elements in the room are out of balance. Chances are it's the color and finishes that are causing the problem.

Photo: Joe Kilanowski

Making a few final adjustments
to this entirely faux painted
structure, which happens to be
the largest theme painted
building in the world.

"A solution to a problem can often be right before you, all that is required is viewing the situation from a different perspective."

– Dino Fauci

5

IDENTIFYING PROBLEM AREAS

(and ways to transform them!)

This just may be the most helpful chapter. Why? Many production homes have problem areas ranging from odd architectural details, to no architectural details, to undesirable materials. Changing the color or the surface of these problem areas to something that works with your design can make all the difference to the harmony of the space. Just by adding highlights, spatter and a wash, you can create a natural looking material which will transform the surface, complement the room, and not be a distraction.

Researching books and even product catalogs for reference photos of the material you are working with is very helpful. Authenticity is a good starting point because I believe natural materials add more life and energy to a space than do plainly painted surfaces. This is not to say you must make your material authentic. You can do whatever you think looks good. This is a personal preference of mine.

Let's take a look at some examples of materials that can be challenging.

BRICKS

I have worked with brick fireplaces my entire career. Some situations called for faux painting existing bricks. This is usually because they need to be returned to their original condition after having been painted a solid color.

In other cases the goal was to change the original color of natural bricks and stone to suit the new design. Yet another situation would be to add life and authenticity to man-made cultured stone.

While working with Disney I mastered the art of painting bricks, stones and many other natural materials. When you see a brick or stone building at one of the theme parks, it is not made of brick. It is generally plaster, fiberglass, or other material which has been painted to look like the real thing. You can use these same techniques to transform undesirable surfaces in your home. The most important thing to consider when painting a brick or stone is keeping it authentic to its shape. For example, large cinderblock would not look authentic if it was painted to look like used brick.

I once saw a space which had a floor to ceiling brick fireplace constructed with geometric shapes, standing in the middle of the room. The floor was 12" x 24" black slate. The walls were white and the bricks were painted a mid to deep-tone grey. The shape and mortar looked to be used brick. Since the space was modern, it worked very well. I understand the designer wanted to work the used brick into the design so painting it was the most economical option. What if the bricks were painted the same grey only with highlights and spatter added? What if the grout was similar to the grout color in the flooring and then an overall aging wash was applied to add realism? Now the bricks would appear to be live bricks and this would give the room the same look, but add additional energy and authenticity. Keep your mind open and look for ways to improve upon your surfaces. Adding just a little more detail can make dramatic differences.

STONE
Real & Cultured

The same exact principles for bricks apply to stones. In recent years builders have been using cultured stone as architectural elements. They are used for siding, arches, quoins and pediments, to name a few. Some of these

look really good and are difficult to distinguish from the real thing. Others do not. When a repeated pattern can be seen and the colors are limited and lifeless it lessens the authenticity of the stone.

At Disney, all of the stones we paint are made from gray cement plaster. The carvers provide us with the stone shapes and textures and I am left to create all the colors from the base coat. In most cases the stones are painted to look real. Other times we paint them whimsical depending on the story. With typical architectural cultured stones, you can work with the colors already provided. You will be surprised what a difference it will make applying some highlights and soft colored washes to random stones. They can be transformed from dull and lifeless to alive, energetic and realistic. This may not be something you would want to try yourself without a little experience under your belt, but there are professional theme artists who can achieve this look.

Knowing what is possible will open your door to infinite possibilities for transforming your space with color and special finishes!!

COLUMNS

Round or Square

Columns of any shape or size can often times be a difficult design challenge, largely because builders use them with no real sense of purpose. At least that is how they appear. The architecture of production homes typically does not support the use of columns. A typical production home with Roman columns in the living room? Why? Regardless of why they are there, something needs to be done with them. But what? That's what this next section is about.

Do you know why you see faux marble columns in private homes? I really don't have an answer myself. I can only speculate. Sometimes if the home is a grand estate, I understand the marble columns are an attempt to create elegance and sophistication. I understand that. I don't necessarily agree with it but I get it. Why don't I agree with it? Think about where marble columns are most commonly used. They are typically used in churches, museums, government buildings, libraries and other large scale buildings. Is this really what you want your home to look like, even if it is a stately manor? I guess some do and I am not here to judge. I just feel the application opportunities are limited and the use of a marble finish on a column should be carefully selected. Other than a situation in which I just described, I can't imagine faux marble ever being a realistic design feature in custom, semi-custom or common production homes. I can't believe they would be authentic in that situation. Unless the goal is to create a *theme*, I prefer to stay true to the authenticity of the architecture and building materials. There are other ways to elevate the décor of any space. It doesn't have to be marble.

Many of the faux marble finishes I see are not very realistic in terms of application methods. It looks like they have been painted and do not represent any real stone. Many times I will see veins and fractures running in every direction and there is no transparency between colors (no depth). I have seen some good work from time to time, but generally most look painted. Faux means fake, so if you can tell it's painted, is it really faux? Anyway, my point here is that in the decision to apply a faux marble finish to columns two things need to be considered. 1) Is the architecture conducive to the finish? 2) Does the person applying the finish possess the skill level to create an authentic finish? If the answer is no to either question, I would select an alternate finish.

So what would be a good alternate finish? If some type of stone is still your most favorable choice, I suggest something soft and light in color with very little movement. If it has to be marble, I suggest something that has subtle movement and veining. In the white tones I like Biancone Carrara, Bianco Arni, Bianco Royal, Crevola D'Ossola and Calacatta Oro. Yellow and tan marbles I like are Biancone, Travertino Bianco, Botticino Semiclassicio and Crema Marafil. Most of the darker marble colors are too variegated for most column applications. The use of softer stones such as limestone, soapstone and travertine are my favorites because they add subtle interest and texture. These stones have a broader usefulness and are less extravagant. If your columns are boxed or square, stacked stone using one of the softer stones I just suggested is an authentic application choice.

So then what should you do with your columns if stone is not an option? If your goal is to accentuate them, I have found the use of accent color works well. You can use a darker color to add strength and support. If your walls are a darker tone, you can use a lighter tone for a nice contrast. So you can go light or dark depending upon your space and what you want to achieve. There are other options such as Venetian and other types of decorative plasters. Usually these materials are only used on columns when the entire space is being treated. By only finishing the columns you create similar problems as we saw in the faux marble.

Here is a final suggestion for those of you whom are adamant about using faux marble. If your columns have a raised base section; you can finish that area as marble and paint the body of the column an accent color. This will add a touch of elegance, without becoming chichi. Remember, less is more. Understate rather than overstate.

PRECAST FIREPLACES SURROUNDS

With most of these pieces the manufacturer tells only half of the story. They provide the shape, but because it doesn't have a finish, quite often it's unclear what the material should be. This is a benefit in my opinion. Why? Because now I can complete the story anyway I see fit.

However, as I have been explaining throughout this book, I want to be true to what material the shape wants to be. Some pieces are so ambiguous that the material they are made from can be almost anything. Others have specific clues that suggest a smaller range of possibilities.

I study each piece looking for specific shapes and details that will direct me to choosing the best and most authentic finish material to apply. This is not a rule, but I find when I stay within the realm of probability, my design choices are more successful.

If the surround has a lot of detail, it may have been carved from a soft stone such as soapstone, alabaster or limestone. Granite is extremely hard which makes fine detail very difficult. If there is not much detail it can most likely be granite or marble such as Italian Carrara which is a favorite among carvers. Wood can be carved into almost any shape so if wood is your choice, the shape and details are less of a consideration. The only limitation with creating a wood finish could be texture. If the texture happens to be unsuitable for a wood finish (a stone texture for example), the surface can always be remedied by smoothing it over with the proper patching material.

I had one project where my client was from New York. His favorite building is The Chrysler Building. It is truly an architectural masterpiece. The fireplace in his space was made from concrete. The shape and surface texture realistically could have been made from stone. I suggested going with faux white granite. My client agreed.

(Chrysler Building painted on canvas and onto faux painted white granite fireplace)

(faux painted white granite)

He then suggested painting The Chrysler Building above the fireplace. This space was a loft and his furnishings were eclectic, so we had a little more freedom to have some fun. The surround protruded two inches from the wall so I suggested painting the building onto a canvas so it would be flush with the surface. This sparked an idea from my client. He wasn't happy with the fireplace opening and wanted to disguise it somehow. He came up with a totally *out-of-the-box* suggestion. Why don't you paint a section of the building directly onto the surround? I would have never thought of this on my own. It was a stretch but thanks to the amazing artistry of Danny Montes whom I commissioned to paint the building, in the end, it worked. The fireplace opening now became a part of the building. It was definitely different but it worked incredibly well with the rest of the décor. Most importantly, it represented my client's personality. We were transforming a box into his personalized environment. This piece transformed the space and became the focal point of the room. This is an example of creating something authentic (white granite) and combining it with a bit of fantasy. In its original condition, the surround was gray, cold and lifeless. In the end, it became something personalized and uniquely special.

If you are going to finish a pre-cast surround, take the time to make it a piece of art. Research the design style and choose a finish that is authentic as much as it suits your décor. I have seen so many of these pieces poorly finished with just a heavy wash. This kind of finish does not represent anything other than a nicely shaped surround with a dirty wash on it. I have also seen surrounds painted white when clearly the piece was asking for, and deserving of a personalized finish. The manufacturer took the time to create a decorative shape. It is up to you to transform it into something special.

FLOORS

Have you ever considered painting your floors? If you have concrete floors, painting them can be a great way to add character to the room. While this is certainly not the mainstream, it can save you a lot of money and turn a difficult challenge into a little gem. The main concerns with painting floors are adhesion and protection. A painted floor can last for years provided the surface is prepared properly and the correct materials are used.

A painted floor is no place to cut corners. Quality materials and application are crucial. Using the best

materials and techniques is always a good policy to follow but for those who choose to skimp on occasion, the floor is not the place to do it. You will lose money and time if you try to economize on a painted floor.

There are so many factors that come into play when painting a concrete floor. A few to consider are pH levels and moisture. It is more important to check these levels when the concrete floor is new or if you live in a moist area. The acceptable levels of these conditions vary from product to product. Be sure to follow the manufacturer's specifications to the letter. Dirt, grease, moisture and other contaminants will affect the paint's bonding capabilities. Make sure your surface is clean and dry before application.

Another area of concern is cracks and holes. There are many excellent patching materials that will remedy either of these problems. I suggest finding a store that specializes in concrete materials.

Another area of concern is cracks and holes. There are many excellent patching materials that will remedy either of these problems. I suggest finding a store that specializes in concrete materials.

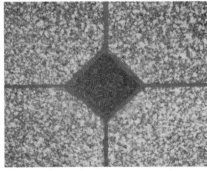

Now that we have preparation and material out of the way, let's talk finishes. The beauty of painting your concrete floor is that it can be anything you can envision. Anything! You can paint wood planks, granite with wood borders and marble granite inlay, limestone, travertine, a trompe l'oeil throw rug, solid colors with modeled patterns, fantasy finishes, murals...the possibilities are endless and can be suited to your particular design.

One important thing to remember when painting a floor is to use as thin of a coat as possible. Why? The thinner the coat, the less chance it has of peeling. There is a school of thought that says to have proper protection, building a thick coating is better. For some applications, steel for example, building up the thickness of a coating can be a benefit. For others it creates more problems than it solves. Thick coatings, especially soft coatings, are more susceptible to peeling. When a harder coating material is applied too heavily it can crack. With most coating applications, especially floors, a few thin coats are best.

Once you have finished applying a spectacular finish to your floor, it's extremely important to apply a protective coating to protect the paint. This coating will help resist scuffs, minor abrasions and provide a cleanable surface, thus adding additional life to the finish. This coating is typically called a clear coat. What you use to protect the finish is just as important as the preparation and primer. Again, do not try to save money with this step. Use the best coating available. The clear coating must be compatible with the materials used to create the finish. For example, if a hard film coating (a solvent-based material) is applied over a soft coating (a water-based material), the clear coat could wrinkle or lift the finish. Also, a soft coating will most likely peel when applied over the top of a hard coating. All of this can be avoided by researching the materials before starting the project. You might consider consulting with flooring contractors and paint stores that primarily service the professional industry to learn what professionals use.

STAIN

Acid & Acrylic

The use of acid stain has been popular for the past few years. It is mostly used in commercial and retail spaces but some homeowners have used it successfully as well.

The below picture is a hand painted finish to simulate an acid stain. Chemical stain was not possible due to previous patching and sealer.

If you decide to use an acid stain, I suggest you hire a professional. Acid stain works best on new concrete. If your slab is 25 years old, you may not get the results you want. The concrete has become dense (cured) and will not accept the stain as it does when it is fresh. There are a few modified acrylic stains on the market. The downside to these products is that they do not penetrate the concrete like acid stains. Always apply a sample in an inconspicuous area such as a closet before attempting the entire surface. The main concerns here are adhesion and color. All concrete surfaces are different. A little research to determine which product will work best in your particular situation is a smart idea.

Once your finish is complete you will want to protect it. I highly suggest you research what professional floor finishers in your area use as a top coat and use those. Make sure everything you use is compatible with each other. Again, apply thin coats and do not get caught up in thinking you need to apply a heavy coat for better protection. Think thin!!

"My concrete floors are covered with tile mastic. There are cracks that need to be repaired and something was spilled before the carpet went down. How can I stain my concrete now?" This scenario would make it virtually impossible to use stain. It would be very expensive to have the floors shot-blasted or resurfaced. If the acid stain look is something you truly desire but either the acid or acrylic stains will not work in your situation for

some reason, there is another option. You can faux paint it to look as if it has been stained.

I once was asked to refinish large planters in an Orange County shopping mall. They doubled as public seating. These planters were originally finished with an acid stain. They had suffered years of abuse from the environment. They suffered from food stains and graffiti, and had also been chipped and broken in areas from local skateboarders.

This is a faux acid stain finish done using acrylic paint. It can also be applied to floors.

The surface could no longer be refinished using a stain of either type. The challenge was to match the planters to other surrounding pieces that shared the same finish. Through the magic of paint (and a little experience) I matched the finish perfectly. How? I properly cleaned the surface and patched the damaged areas. I then primed the entire surface using a high grade acrylic concrete primer. Next I applied an acrylic base coat that was as close to the existing color. I mixed up four different colors to use as washes. These washes mimicked the effects of the stain. I then sealed the entire surface with a water-based two-part urethane. This same treatment can be applied to your floors or any surface where this particular finish is desired.

CEILINGS

When I think of one of the most popular problem areas in older homes, acoustic (cottage cheese) ceilings come to mind. I only have one suggestion for this application: REMOVE IT. I find nothing appealing about an acoustic ceiling. All it will do is date your home and make it look dirty. Even if they have been previously painted, they can be removed. This is a physical and messy job. Many homeowners take this job on themselves, but unless you feel you are up to the task, hire a pro to do it. It could prove to be well worth the expense.

Aside from the challenges of acoustic ceilings, or poorly textured ceilings, most people do not give ceilings much thought. Ceilings are one of the biggest areas in a room. They can add so much to the feel of a room. It all depends upon your architecture. High ceilings, low ceilings, wood ceilings, dome ceilings, textured ceilings. So what do you do with your ceiling? Most people paint them white. Some paint them the same color as the walls and others paint them darker than the walls. There is no rule here. It's about whatever works with the space. As I have been repeatedly saying, it depends on lighting, architecture, surfaces furnishings, and your design goals.

What if you have a wood ceiling and it has been painted but you wish it could be wood again? What are your options? How about chemical removers? No thank you. What about a heat gun? That can produce toxic fumes, so again, no thank you. Sandblasting? Well this is a faster method but it destroys the wood's surface. Unless you want a sandblasted look, this may not be a great option either. So, how do you transform a painted wood ceiling back to its original condition while keeping the integrity of the wood's surface intact? With a few steps you can faux paint your ceiling to look like wood again. While you may not be able to do it yourself, understand that this is an option. A faux wood finish can be a substantial time and money saver.

I know, you might be thinking faux finishes are expensive, especially wood grain finishes. You could be right, but when you weigh it against the other options, and once you realize some tricks to painting a faux wood ceiling, you might just change your mind.

Why? Because the ceiling will not be viewed at close proximity, the level of detail required is far less than a surface you can touch and view up close. It is much easier to fool the eye from a distance.

I will use the movie industry to help explain my point. Much of what you see in movies and television sets has been faux painted. The wood paneling or marble walls, wood doors, bricks, and stones in the background are in most cases faux painted. If you were to stand directly in front of these finishes, it would be very obvious they are painted. The artists are required to exaggerate the features of the material in order for the camera to read the finish. Now, to finish your wood ceiling to be authentic as well as affordable, blending the techniques used for movie sets with those used for fine faux finishing is the trick to achieving the look you want in a reasonable amount of time and expense

Wood graining your ceiling is a cost saving choice that will also be a great conversation piece. When you tell people the wood grain is faux painted they will be blown away! I recently faux painted ceramic mosaic tiles on the ceiling of a wine room I designed. When people see it, they love it. They say to my client, "Wow, I can't believe you put mosaic in here. It's beautiful!" Then when they tell them it's painted, they are completely in awe! For an example of this finish please visit dinofauci.com

EMBOSSED WALLPAPER

Installing embossed wallpaper on the ceiling? REALLY? Absolutely! There are some really nice patterns available that when properly painted look amazing.

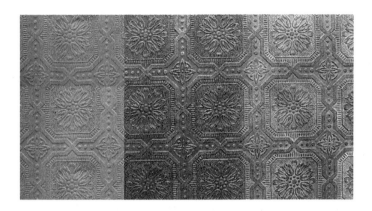

I have made some look like copper, brass, and leather. They can be solidly painted and aged or just painted a single color.

Embossed wallpaper adds texture and a level of sophistication. It is a great way to give character to a bar, den, reading room, or even a kitchen. If you desire a coffered ceiling you can install the embossed paper and paint it to look like aged copper. I have also used embossed wall paper for wainscot. It is really a great material that provides numerous possibilities.

COUNTERTOPS and TABLE TOPS

I have been asked so many times, "Can you paint tile or Formica?" The answer is always, "Yes but you have to

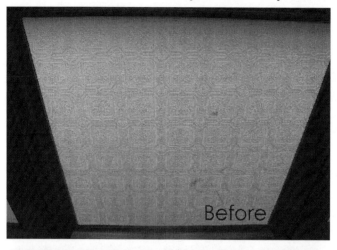

Before

understand that it will scratch off eventually." These surfaces are difficult to paint but there are some products which will work. ALWAYS do a test on a similar piece. If you can scratch it off with your finger nail after it is cured, try a different product or scrap the idea. If on the other hand you are successful with adhesion, you can make your countertop look like anything you want. My workbench in my garage is faux granite! Everyone thinks it's real. I also have a piece of furniture the top of which I faux painted in green marble. I even had a marble installer comment on what a nice piece of marble it was. The secret here is the same as any coating: surface prep and quality top coat (clear coat). If you are considering painting your kitchen counters (I do not recommend this for maintenance reasons), be sure you use a non-toxic material and be careful not to use that surface for cutting.

If you are going to paint tiles, I suggest you sand and clean the surface thoroughly, apply the proper primer, then paint the grout color. Then paint each tile separately. I am not fond of the grout and tiles all painted the same color. Make it look real. Otherwise it looks like you painted your tile! Painting tile and grout together as one solid color is not a quality look. It's much better to take the time and create a realistic finish. To make your tiles look even more believable, try adding highlights and color washes over them. This will give them an authentic ceramic appearance. When doing this you may have to go back and touch up the grout color. If ceramic is not going to work, you can add some texture with a sea sponge to make them look like stone. If you take the time to pay attention to detail, you will enjoy the rewards when finished. For examples of faux painted wood ceilings, embossed wallpaper ceilings and painted tiles, please visit my website at: dinofauci.com

"Color selection is not a decision, it's a realization."

– Dino Fauci

I transformed a rather uninteresting space into an implied Irish Pub atmosphere that is now fun and exciting. This was done with only color and specialty finishes with the existing architecture and surfaces. I used plaster and faux paint techniques to create dimensional bricks at flanking walls at the bar. Faux painted copper ceiling, aged patina walls and dark antique glaze applied to existing woodwork all added to the authenticity of the environment.

6

CREATING A THEME

Storytelling

Paint is to the theme painter,
what words are to the poet.

The professional description of my position when I work with Walt Disney Imagineering is Production Designer/Art Director. But if you ask me what my job is at Disney, I will tell you that I am a *storyteller*. My job is to tell a story with paint and textures rather than words. I'll use my latest project, Tower of Terror at Tokyo Disney Sea as an example. It is the largest theme painted building to date. The Tower had a story that needed to be presented in paint and other materials. The story said that when this structure was originally built it was a grand hotel made from the finest materials available at the time. The hotel's owner had used it to showcase many ancient artifacts which he had collected from all over the world. One night, there was a mysterious explosion in one of the elevators destroying a few of the floors that exposed the elevator lobbies to the outside. This event caused the hotel to close. Over the years due to being abandoned and exposed to the elements, the building had become very run down and decrepit.

The first step was to create the building materials. Materials that needed to be replicated included a copper roof, three types of bricks, limestone, brownstone, sandstone, granite, travertine, laterite, wood, bronze, brass, ancient tiles, wallpaper, broken concrete, granite floors with accent inlay, fabrics and a skylight. The skylight was actually a shroud to hide mechanical equipment and was made from an opaque material which needed to look like real glass.

Once these materials were created, I had to imagine how time and exposure would affect this building in all areas, including inside the elevator shafts. I also had to consider how each material would age due to its location. How should ancient artifacts that were centuries old look?

Defining these finishes is crucial to portraying a believable story. My job was not only to develop these finishes but to direct my team of over a hundred very talented theme painters to produce a faux / theme painted building that told this story. The Tower of Terror was a huge success because the story that my team told in paint was believable and authentic. I am so proud of this project and all of the amazingly talented people it took to create it.

A theme is a story. Whether you are designing your living room or a theme park, you are telling a story. You have to decide what story you are going to tell. Your goal is to have the viewer believe the story you have created. When we were finished with Tower, the thought of paint never even passes the viewers minds. They see a fifteen story building that looks like it has been there for a very long time. They know it's a theme park. They know it is an attraction, and yet they believe the hotel's story!

SELECTING A THEME

When you select a theme for your home, office or place of business, it is very important that you stay authentic. I keep bringing this up because it is your guide to a successful design. With every idea you have to stop and ask yourself, "Why?" Why would that be there? What should it really look like? Does it add value to the design or is it a distraction?

Selecting a theme for your space can be done in a number of ways. One of the easiest ways to come up with a theme is to reinforce the definitive architectural style of your home. Many of the homes here in California are built in a Spanish or Mediterranean influence. It is much easier to create an authentic design for these homes because the shapes are in place. We also have Bungalows and Craftsman homes. There are plenty of authentic reference materials to properly create time period designs with these homes as well.

In the South, the traditional *Five, Four and a Door* style homes are abundant. As with the California home styles, there are plenty of reference materials to assist you with your design. But what if your home has no particular style? It is difficult to transform a 70's style production home into a Spanish Hacienda, European Chateau or West Indies Beach House, and have it look authentic. So what to do? Remodel? You most certainly can but that is a different book. The idea here is for you to transform your home without having to do that.

Do you want to theme the entire house or just one room? Understand your architecture and understand your surfaces (flooring, countertops, shower enclosures etc.) If you are not changing them they become part of the design. Look for architectural elements such as columns, posts, arches, soffits, beams and moldings. These can be used to make your theme more authentic. If no particular style is represented, these elements can be used as focal points. If they are in fact problem areas in your design, find ways to minimize their impact.

My suggestions so far have been to keep within your style of architecture, but what if you just want to have some fun? Maybe you are into sailing, airplanes, or fishing.

Perhaps you have an array of collectibles. You can build a theme around these. Selecting a room in your home and creating a theme can be fun and a nice getaway from the stress of everyday life. How about a tropical cabana? That could work really well in Minnesota where it is 40 below in the winter. How about creating a wine cellar? Make the room feel like you are in the basement of an old castle complete with aged stone walls. You could add effloresce leaching, some moss in the corners, rustic wood cabinets and a time period light fixture. You can even pull the carpet and utilize the concrete floor. Paint the floor faux castle stone or wood planking! How about a country side winery with European plaster walls, some break away areas, maybe a trompe l'oeil painting on the wall or a fresco?

Creating a theme in one room is much more practical than in an entire home. It can enrich the time you, your family and your friends spend in your home. Our homes are our castles. This is a fun way to make it really feel like one.

MAKING IT AUTHENTIC

I know, I know, I keep reminding you to make sure everything you do is authentic. I understand there may not be a budget to make it 100% authentic, which is fine. What ever decision you make, make it with a clear understanding of why it should be there. Be selective. When you create a finish, make it as convincing as possible. In all seriousness, if you are not going to do it right, why bother?

The point of establishing a theme is to trick the viewer into believing what they see is real. If viewers specifically notice what was done on your theme, then the theme isn't effective. A poorly applied theme will cause visitors to spend their time analyzing the badly executed work rather than appreciating the theme. You want to create a feeling and a mood without calling attention to the finishes or how they were achieved. We want the viewer to appreciate that it is there, not ask why it is there.

If cost is an issue, it is better to do your theme one section at a time and do it right than to rush through it and end up being less than 100% satisfied with the results. I am sure seasoned designers and artists may agree with my philosophy and think what I'm saying is obvious. For some of you however, it may not be that obvious. My father told me a story once about how his father would ask him; "Did you tell them? All you can do is let them know." So now, following in family footsteps, I told you, even if it is something you already know.

DON'T OVERSTATE

I strongly recommend keeping your designs understated. I have already discussed this in previous chapters but I can't emphasize this enough. Many times theme and character finishes are overstated. Focus on keeping the *volume* down. In other words, bigger, brighter and louder is great for an amusement park. In your home, subtle is best. Some examples of overkill include art that is too ostentatious, too large or too bright for the space, frames which are too ornate, colors which are too bright or too dark, furniture which is too large for the room, or even having too much furniture.

Less is more. I first learned this when I became a drummer many years ago. Remember Keith Moon?

Keith Moon was a bombastic drummer for the English rock band The Who. At first I really liked the way he played. He played a drum fill almost every two bars, which for a beginning drummer was very exciting. I started out playing in the same way. As I matured I learned this style of playing is far too much for most circumstances. Keith's busy, over the top style worked really well for that unique situation. Keith's style was perfect for The Who's music. Once Keith was gone, anyone filling his seat would have to play exactly like him or the music would not sound the same. His style was the signature drum sound of that band. Keith played too much and too often only by comparison. For example, if Moon played with any other band such as The Rolling Stones or The Beatles, he would not have fit in.

Now, look at Charlie Watts, drummer for the Rolling Stones. He has a distinctive style, yet his style could blend in with many other bands. Watts played fewer notes which would be more appropriate for numerous situations. So what's the point? Keith Moon as great as he was, played SO MANY notes that everything he played blended together. His creativity actually loses value because it's all big and busy. Watts on the other hand plays fewer notes so when he makes a statement with a drum fill or accent, it stands out and is noted as something special. This example crosses into all levels of design and art.

When you are designing or creating a theme, you want to be careful not to add too much. One of the phrases I use everyday is: "You can always add to a design, but it is much more difficult to take away." Get the basic design intent established. Once you have that, you can start to build slowly. Once you get to a certain level, STOP and step back. How does it look? More importantly, how does it feel? Remember, you are creating a theme but true success is achieved when your theme stops being a visual attraction and becomes a feeling. When you feel like you are there, you are there.

Themed Pizza Restaurant (Extreme Pizza) where we created a plaster and paint rockwork wall.

Smokey aged walls, ceiling, and faux copper ceiling over the bar and faux bricks complete the theme of this Irish Pub setting in my client's home.

Classic Simplicity

7

CLASSICAL VS. TRENDY

Traditional vs. Modern

Remember in the 80's when everyone was decorating with a *South Western* style? Everything was aqua and peach pastels. That lasted for a few years then it was gone. It was trendy and did not last. We all need to have a little fun but when we are talking about the expense of decorating your home, cost is a huge factor. If you have unlimited funds, go ahead and redecorate every year with the latest trendy style. (If you do this, please contact me at dinofauci.com). I'm not saying stay away from trendy styles. However, understanding the differences between the trendy and classic can help you make an informed decision that could save you the cost and effort of having to remodel often.

Most of us need to choose wisely so we can get many years of enjoyment from our design. Choosing a color or finish because everyone else is doing it can be a huge mistake unless you absolutely love that style. I am using South Western as an example because I found so many people decorating in this theme with no personal or architectural connection. It was just popular at the time.

Trendy could have the potential of becoming a theme in the future. Shag carpeting and earth-tone colors like harvest gold, avocado green and burnt orange, are currently making a comeback in some areas. So if you decide to go trendy and happen to keep it that way, in about thirty years your home may have a theme! Seriously, trendy is fun, hip, and if done with care and attention to quality, it will offer you years of enjoyment. But even so, if the style does not truly represent your architecture or your lifestyle, you may quickly grow tired of it.

Some may view *classical* as safe, boring, drab and lifeless. I completely disagree. Simplicity can, and usually does, have a powerful effect. It all depends on how it is done and if what is done has a meaning. While I was living in Japan, I quickly came to appreciate the Japanese culture and traditional (classical) architecture. Every material used has meaning. A room may have only a few items in it, but each item is extremely important. I found this to be very powerful. There was a small room with nothing in it except one art piece and an orchid hanging on the wall. It was elegance in its simplest form. This is not for everyone but it struck a chord with me.

Classical elegance in any tradition can be very dynamic and meaningful. You do not need to purchase expensive pieces to create the look you desire. Just be selective in your choices. Do some research on the history of the style. More importantly, I recommend doing some research on what is genuinely important to you.

Our tastes change throughout our lives. Even if you decide to be more traditional, there is no guarantee you will not grow tired of that as well. Before embarking on a major style change, take some time to decide what's really important to you. What makes you feel good? Stay true to yourself and you will get the most enjoyment from your new space. At the end of the day, the design should reflect you. You should connect with your space. Your space is your personal refuge.

BRINGING IT ALL TOGETHER

When I design for my clients, I spend a lot of time with them so I can understand their personalities, their lifestyle, and what matters most to them in their living environment. Through this process it is not only me who learns something, the owners of the space learn a lot about themselves too. This is what makes my designs successful.

It is not about me, it is about you or the owner of the space. I need to know what is important to that person. Aside from my design and finishing talents, the most important tools for me are my ears. If I do not hear the client, I cannot please them. I cannot tell you how many times I have discovered new ideas by listening to my clients. Everyone is different so by listening, I develop new ideas and how to improve upon what I know. Having a discussion with family, friends or a designer about what would make you happier in your home will help you make new discoveries as well.

It's easy to get stuck on one thing or a particular style. It's very important to get past this. I always keep an open mind and I never get offended when someone does not like one of my suggestions. Why? It's only a suggestion. There have been times when I would submit a sample and the client did not feel a connection to it, I was not offended. Why not? The quality of the work was not in question; the sample just did not have any particular meaning to them. How can anyone be offended by that? I am not. It only means I need to dig a little deeper into their desire to find something they will connect with.

Many people, maybe even you, are not sure what they want. Some do not even know what they like until they see it. Others know what they want, but do not know how to achieve it. My job, as the artist/designer, is to help them discover what they like, what they want, and then figure out a way to bring it all together. Your responsibility, if doing this on your own, or even with a designer, is to discover what you connect with. Discovering what connects you to your environment will give your project the best possible chance for a successful design.

The goal is to have the finished project be a personalized environment. My finished projects are not created only by me. I do not create them on my own. I cannot create any of these projects exactly the same way without the owner's input. Oh sure, I could definitely create a dynamic space on my own but that's not why they hire me. When I leave, I need to leave behind something that they will appreciate and resonate with every single day. It's only through them, that I can truly be successful.

The key to transforming your home into a personalized environment is to go through these steps on your own. Spend time evaluating everything I have talked about: color, special finishes (ask if they will really add value), your architecture (its style, advantages, disadvantages, problem areas, utilization of hidden elements), and possible themes (or not). Most importantly, spend time alone in your environment to feel the space and envision the possibilities.

Utilize personal items to
create your personalized environment.

8

HOME SHOPPING

This chapter is not about shopping for a home. Instead it's about shopping within your home! Many people have some hidden treasures inside their homes and don't even know it. When you are looking for ways to change your environment, shopping for these hidden treasures in your home is a great way to start. You just need to look at things in a different way. Remember my opening quote? *"When you open your mind, you open your eyes and allow yourself to see things you never saw before. When you learn that everything in life is art, you then begin to appreciate everything old in a new way."*

FURNITURE

You might be tired of some of your furniture and think it needs to be replaced. A fresh eye upon it may see it in a different light. Think of ways it could look different. It may only need to be refinished. Maybe the addition of some hand painted design would change its character. Try a faux painted marble top or wood grain inlay to make it new again.

You will be surprised what a little imagination can do to transform furniture. For example: I bought an old antique hutch that was a steal. It consisted of a cabinet base with two doors and two drawers. The upper piece was a frame with a mirror back, spindles on the sides and a small shelf. It was a very nice looking piece. It was stained almost black and the two cabinet doors at the bottom were severely warped. I had new doors made which was not expensive. I decided to paint the piece rather than strip off the old finish because this would go with the rest of the items in the room. I painted it white and sanded back the finish, exposing the wood underneath in areas that would naturally become worn. The room where this hutch would be placed had soft yellow and green accents. I used those colors on some of the ornate details to add some additional interest. I then applied a soft aging wash to finish the story of this piece being very old and heavily used.

The cabinet top was not very interesting and I knew it needed something special to bring this piece alive. After some thought, a slab of dark green marble came to mind.

I purchased a beautiful piece of green marble for $1500.00. No not really, but instead I painted the top to look like expensive green marble. Everyone that sees this piece just raves about it. They also believe the marble to be real. I took a piece of furniture that was headed for the trash and turned it into something special. And so can you!

Here's another example of giving your furniture a new look. A client of mine had a beautiful armoire. The problem was it was finished in the 80's. Can you guess what type of finish it had? Yes, it was whitewashed. They recently had purchased new bedroom furniture and the dated finish on the armoire was not going to work. They loved the cabinet but did not want to go to the expense to have it stripped and refinished. I offered a solution to their problem. I suggested applying a colored glaze over the existing finish. With just a few coats (and a little skill), I was able to transform a dated finish into a

beautiful traditional finish. It looks as if it were stained to match their new furniture. By using the glaze, I was able to salvage the natural wood grain. This gave my finish authenticity. So unless you were told how it was finished, you would think it was a traditionally stained piece.

Do you have some furniture in your home or office that you are tired of? Thinking of throwing them away? Before you do, reviving their life and usefulness can be as simple as moving them around or giving them a new finish. You will be surprised what a little imagination can do for these tired pieces. I once made a cardboard box into a marble coffee table, so I know your furniture can be transformed into something else. You just need to start looking and start imagining.

MIRRORS AND FRAMES

How about that mirror or picture frame that's just not working anymore? I have transformed a number of these pieces with little effort and you can too. How often do you see those extremely ornate gold frames? I do not want to offend anyone, but most of these are unattractive. They are too ostentatious, too bright and too busy. While you cannot change the fact they are ornate, you can soften the effect by toning down the color with glazes. Another way is to paint them solid and add highlights to the raised areas.

Other frames that may be plain or lifeless can be brought to life with a different finish. Today there are great acrylic metallic paint, stencil and glue-on (appliqué) products. All of these can add new life to a lifeless frame. These projects are fun and rewarding.

LAMPS AND LIGHTING FIXTURES

Do you have a lamps or lighting fixtures that are tired or dated? Why not paint them? I have refinished many different styles of lighting fixtures ranging from table lamps to chandeliers. You would be amazed how simple

it is to transform a lamp. Not all lighting fixtures can be re-painted with any type of paint. If you are painting a fixture that gets warm, be sure to use a heat-tolerant paint. Using an acrylic paint in this case can cause the material to burn. Check the flash point of the paint before using it. Once you are sure which paint to use, a new finish on a light fixture can be a light-saver. I understand some fixtures just need to go away, but if you have something you can work with, give it a try before you toss it in the donation box.

INTERIOR AND EXTERIOR
FLOWER POTS AND PLANTERS

Do you have undesirable flower pots in your home? Do you search endlessly at home centers for a flower pot style and finish you like? Most of these pots can be painted. I have done it many times. This is something that

is easy and fun to do. From aged finishes to fantasy, the options are limitless. I often find a pot or planter where the style is perfect but the finish is not desirable. I don't let that discourage me. I'll just paint it they way I want it to look.

If the pot is terracotta or porous stone, I recommend that the interior side of the pot be properly sealed. This will naturally help prevent any moisture from penetrating and lifting the finish. If the pot or planter is plastic, it can be painted. Be sure to lightly scuff the surface, remove the dust and then wipe clean using a mild solvent such as acetone. Be sure to use a high quality primer made specifically for plastics. Once you have completed your

finish, apply a couple thin coats of an acrylic clear. These come in a variety of sheens ranging from flat to gloss. If your pots or planters will be outside, be sure to use a clear coat rated for exterior (UV Inhibitor).

Note: Planters that have been fired with a ceramic glaze should not be painted. There are primers that claim to adhere to ceramic surfaces, however since the planter holds moist material, the chance of the coating failing is much greater.

PHOTOS, CERTIFICATES OF RECOGNITION, CHILDREN'S ARTWORK

Most of our photos are in albums or on our computers. Your certificates of recognition may be in a typical black frame or in a drawer. The kids' art is on the refrigerator with magnets from the local realtor. Many times family photos are in a frame sitting on a shelf or a coffee table or perhaps hanging on the wall. This seems to be a typical way of displaying these photos.

These items are just displayed as pictures not art. Now, what if you looked at these photos, certificates and kids' art as artwork? These are images of people and places that are important to you. They have meaning. No picture, painting or piece of art you would purchase is as important as these items. Sure a Picasso would be nice, but he is not your child. Why not celebrate their talent? A photograph of a place you visited, and the photo you took of that place means more to you than some random photo someone else took...right? Seeing these items in a different way will reveal their enormous value to you and others. If these items are mounted and displayed properly, you will have a unique and highly valuable piece of art to share.

Here is an example. I spent a lot of time looking for some authentic Japanese art pieces for my own home. Most of what I found was very expensive or really inexpensive, and it looked like it. I did not want a cheap looking piece just because it was Japanese style. I wanted the piece to have meaning. Everything I was looking at had no meaning or value to me. Then it hit me. I have hundreds of photos I had taken while I was living in Japan. I selected a few that I really liked. I used Photoshop to turn them from color to black and white prints. I also used the program to age them slightly. The pictures were taken of temples in Kyoto, so the subjects are hundreds of years old. Changing to black and white and aging them added additional character. I printed them and mounted them in Asian style frames complete with quality matting. This gave the photos a level of sophistication that just placing them in an ordinary picture frame never could.

They are now hanging in my home and I love looking at them everyday. They keep me connected to a place that is important to me. It was very inexpensive, fun to do and most importantly, I have a connection to these places because I was there. You can do the same and turn your vacation photos, family gathering, sporting event, child's activities or pet photos into genuine artwork. If you are not computer savvy, you may have a friend or family member who is.

Photos can be scanned to digitize them. You can do it yourself or take them to a digital photo lab where they will do it for you. The point is, you will have a unique piece of art that has great meaning to you and your family for little expense. You will be surprised how good your three year old child's art piece will look when it is matted and properly framed.

OLD TOOLS, TIME PIECES, WRITING UTENSILS, ALBUM COVERS, MAGAZINE COVERS, NEWSPAPER HEADLINES

Your great grandfather's pocket watch may be laying in a box somewhere, unappreciated. Why not frame it? It really is a piece of art. Look at the craftsmanship and the engineering which went into creating it. We are so conditioned into thinking paintings, sculptures and other people's photography are art. Not me; I see everything as art. Just look around you. Everything you see is an art form. Be it God's art or man-made. Everything we have in our lives was imagined, designed and crafted. Isn't that art?

If something has meaning to you, it can be displayed as art. I have my Van Halen 1984 album that was autographed to me nicely framed and hanging in my office. It sits beside a framed autographed copy of the November 1988 magazine cover of Modern Drummer featuring the late, great, Jeff Porcaro. To me this is art. These items have special meaning. I get to see them everyday. I have displayed them as art because they truly are.

The magazine cover was shot by a professional photographer that took special interest in making this shot the best of their ability. The same is true of the album cover. I am sure there were many hours laboring over that image and layout. It was created by an artist. It may be just an album cover to some or a magazine cover to others. Your grandfather's watch may be just a watch to some but these pieces are special to those that see them and have a connection to them. Find what you are connected to and make that your art.

NATURAL FINDS
(Driftwood, Rocks, Autumn Leaves)

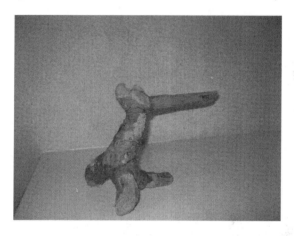

God's art is some of the best I have seen. Natural items provide a great opportunity to have artwork in your home. I do not have a lot in my home, but I do have a few pieces. I have an assortment of autumn leaves nicely framed in my guest room which was made by a special friend. I found a piece of driftwood that reminds me of a unicorn. I have a few beautiful rocks from a special location. I also have two seashells on my desk that were given to me by two children living on Beqa Island in Fiji as a gesture of gratitude for the candy we brought them. These seashells are profoundly special.

As simple as these objects are, they remind me of nature, what I was doing when I discovered them and whom I was with at the time. Some remind me of the person who gave them to me. These items have meaning to me, so I use them in my design.

Go up in your rafters, go into the garage and closets and dig through old boxes. Looking at things in a different way will shed new light onto a once forgotten or overlooked object. You will be surprised at the treasures you have right in your own home. All it takes is a little imagination. Even if you choose not to use any of these suggestions for your own home, I hope these ideas will unlock your vision and allow you to appreciate things you didn't notice before. I feel fortunate to see the artistry in everything. Even in a rock. So go shopping in your home and have fun!

"Paint is the most economical way to transform your space. Even the most modest house can become an exquisite home through proper color coordination and personal flair."

– Dino Fauci

Dino applying an aging finish to Mitch's Java & Jazz in Newhall, CA.

9

DIY

DO IT YOURSELF

"Take the time to do it right the first time, because there always seems to be enough time to do it right the second."

I am not sure where this quote originated. All I know is my father drilled it into my head while growing up.

In this chapter I focus on important tips to make your project safer, less stressful, more economical and much more successful. This will not be a step-by-step or how-to chapter. While I feel it is important you know how to paint, this book is not intended to go through the painting process step by step. I will however give you some professional knowledge so if you decide to tackle your own project or need to communicate with a contractor about your project, you will have some valuable tips to assist you.

Many people do not like to paint. This is something I never understood. Since I was a small child I always loved to paint. I remember going to work at my father's paint shop. He would have me clean up the shop and mix all the partially full gallon paint cans together into five gallon buckets. Sometimes I would put my hand in the paint, squeeze my fist and let the paint ooze through my fingers. I was a weird kid, okay? I love texture! I once asked my dad if he could bring all the paint home and fill up our swimming pool. You can guess his answer. Hey, I was a kid. The secret to painting with success is you need to at least enjoy it. Otherwise it will be torture.

If you can change how you feel about painting, you just may learn to enjoy it. If you agree to do that, I will share some trade secrets with you that will make the experience an enjoyable one. Yes, an ENJOYABLE one.

SURFACE PREPARATION

"A FINISHED PRODUCT IS ONLY AS GOOD AS THE PREPARATION" – How true this statement is, how far too often is ignored.

Surface preparation is as everyone knows, the most important step of any paint job. Yes, it is something, everyone knows, but is also the most disliked aspect of the process. Due to the lack of love for this procedure, many skip the necessary steps and find the final coat application more difficult. This ends up being the cause for most paint failures.

If a surface is not prepared properly, nothing will be right from that point forward. Any imperfections left in the preparation process will be present in the final product. Just for the record, paint does not fill small holes. They need to be filled with patching compound before you begin painting. Glossy surfaces need to be sanded or the primer or paint will not adhere properly. Raw surfaces need to have the appropriate primer applied first. Do not try to eliminate these steps. If you do, it will cost you. Do it right the first time because there always seems to be enough time to do it right the second!

JOB SITE PREPARATION

Preparing your job site is just as important as preparing your surfaces. Why? If your job site is not prepared properly, you will be frustrated from start to finish. How should you get prepared? Start by what is known in the trades as, *setting up shop*. A shop is where you will store all your tools and materials during the project. For obvious reasons, I like to keep this as close to the work area as possible.

I first start by laying a piece of 1mm plastic down, cut to the size of my *shop* drop cloth. Then I place a heavy drop-cloth over the plastic. I do this in the event a paint can or other liquid is tipped over. The plastic will prevent seepage and damage of the floor below. I then place all my materials and tools on the cloth in an orderly fashion. I make sure to keep the primer and paints separate from the tools. A neat shop will help you stay organized and save time.

Next I move the furniture into the center of the room or out of the room if possible. In the case of extensive sanding, I will cover the furniture with two layers of plastic. Why? Because the dust will settle on the top layer of plastic so when the plastic is removed the dust is less likely to stir up and settle on the furniture. Once the furniture is covered, I then dust the walls, window sills and baseboards. Next, I vacuum or sweep the floor. Now I have a clean environment to work in. If you follow these simple steps, you will too!

TIME SAVING TIPS –
MASKING THE CARPETS AND BASEBOARDS

If you are painting your baseboards and have carpeting, use two inch masking tape to protect the carpet. Pull two to three feet of tape off the roll leaving it attached to the roll. Place the tape on the carpet next to the baseboard with approximately 1/8th inch of tape on the bottom of the baseboard. Now, tuck the 1/8th inch piece of tape under the base providing a barrier between the bottom of the base and the carpet. This will serve two functions. The width of the tape will help protect the carpeting in case there are any voids in the drop cloths. Secondly, you will have protection when you paint the base. I still do this method even when I am not painting the base to protect the carpeting.

After the carpet is protected I use one inch tape and mask the top of the baseboard. This also serves two functions. The primary function is protection from the roller spatter. You do not want dried roller spatter on your baseboards. When you paint the base it will look like you painted over sand. And you certainly do not want to sand it off later. Mask it first! The second function is to expedite the use of the paint brush when cutting-in the wall color. Make sure to not place a fully-loaded paint brush onto the tape. Start by applying the paint to the wall about two inches above the baseboard and work the paint in a horizontal motion bringing the paint down to the baseboard. This is the only time I use tape is to cut up to the trim. Why? Because if the paint seeps under the tape (and it almost always does), I am painting the baseboards anyway. I will explain this in more detail in the next chapter.

PROTECTING THE FLOORS

I prefer to use 4' X 12' canvas runners with a rubberized bottom. These have a double function. The rubberized bottom prevents liquids from seeping through. When using these on hardwood or tile floors, they also minimize slipping. If you do not want to purchase these runners, I suggest you place plastic down first, then cover with an old sheet or what ever you choose to use as a drop-cloth. If you use an old bed sheet and step on wet paint droppings, it will soak into the carpet below if there is no plastic barrier.

CAUTION:

When using plastic sheeting to cover walls, floors, ceiling, furniture and fixtures:

- Never place on any living thing. This means plants, shrubs, grass, people, pets, etc.

- Never cut material directly on the floor using a razor blade, knife, or other sharp   tool.

- Always cut material away from your person and other surfaces.

- Always make sure material is overlapped and taped securely to avoid seepage.

- Always make sure plastic is securely fastened to prevent tripping.

When using drop cloths and runners to cover floors and furnishings:

- Keep cloth flat and free from voids or raised areas.

- When placed on wood or tile floors, make sure the cloth is secure from slippage (Never place tape on a wood floor. NO EXCEPTIONS, THE TAPE CAN REMOVE THE FLOOR FINISH.)

- Always keep wet side against the wall which will minimize the chance of stepping into wet material and tracking paint onto unprotected areas.

- Always keep one side clean. A drop cloth should always have one clean side. Only one side should have paint on it.

- When working with washes, plastic must be used under the drop cloth. It must also be securely fastened.

- When folding the drop clothes, be sure to fold them end-to-end. This will keep the wet edge against itself while keeping the drop cloth in pristine condition allowing you to work more efficiently.

When working with ladders:

- Always move ladders with two hands.

- Never move a ladder with a paint can on the ladder shelf.

- Always keep tools and paint cans away from ladders.

- Always make sure ladders are on a solid, level and non-slip surface.

- Keep fingers on the outside of the rails of extension ladders.

- Never step on the top step of a ladder and do not use the shelf as a step.

- Never overreach while on a ladder.

A Quick Story About
Overreaching on a Ladder

It was one of my typical high school weekends which I spent working for my father. Our crew was painting a parking garage. I was assigned to prep work, which meant I had to clean all the dirt off the suspended pipes which ran throughout the garage. Sounds fun I know! And to think I still wanted to peruse a career in painting after that…hmmm. Anyway, I was working on a 12 foot ladder. I wanted to clean a little more of this pipe before having to go down and move the ladder. I was holding on to a pipe and placed one foot on another pipe so I could lean out. I reached so far that now I had to push off the pipe to get myself back onto the ladder. In doing this I tipped the ladder and was beginning to fall. I quickly reached for the pipe to save myself. Well the pipe saved me from falling, but it happened to be a fire sprinkler pipe. The mounting system it was attached to pulled loose from the ceiling. As the pipe bent, bringing me safely to the ground, it broke! Water was free flowing and we could not get it to shut off. This happened on the first level so the water started to flow to the lower levels. That was not the biggest problem. It was now flowing into the lobby of the building. It seemed like eternity before the fire department arrived to shut it off.

Thankfully I was not hurt, but I did do some damage and caused unnecessary stress to my father, the building manager, the fire department and our crew. The only good that came of it was the lesson I learned and the opportunity to share this story. I hope it prevents you from over-reaching and having an accident.

Please be careful!

ACCESS

Keeping your job site clean and clear of debris will allow you to work more efficiently and safely. When you are finished using a tool, return it to the staging area. Now you know where to find it and will not trip on it.

Before moving the furniture into the center of the room, make sure you have proper access with your ladders. You do not want to be moving furniture once you have started working. Some areas could be tight, but try to leave at least six feet of space between the wall and the furniture.

SAFETY

Painting is often viewed as difficult work but often not very dangerous. I have experience to the contrary. Years ago I was painting the exterior of a Victorian home. These homes have a very steeply pitched roof. The builder had made what is called *ladder cleats*. These are blocks of wood with nails at the bottom. It's necessary to slam the blocks onto the shingles forcing the nails into the roofing material creating a level surface on which to place the ladder. This proved to be not such a safe system. I was on the roof, leaving the ladder to climb onto the second story roof. At that moment I was thinking, "I sure hope the ladder doesn't slip!" Well, just then the ladder cleats slipped away. In the blink of an eye, I was on the ground. Luckily, I was able to ride the ladder down like a snow sled. The accident left me only scraped and bruised. I actually went right back to work but this could have been much more serious. Any time you are using an extension ladder (or any ladder) that is on a slippery or angled surface, never go on the ladder unless you have someone footing the ladder. Footing the ladder occurs when a person places their feet behind the feet of the ladder to create stability. This will prevent the ladder from slipping.

Question: What's more dangerous a two foot step ladder, or a sixteen foot extension ladder? Answer: They are both equally as dangerous. I can prove it! I was applying an aging finish on kitchen cabinets for a remodeled home. At this point the owners had started moving their things back into the home. I had not noticed a new throw rug they placed between the island and the refrigerator. I placed my runner directly over it. When I was stepping off the 2' step ladder, I was on top of the throw rug and it slipped. I was thrown backwards against the marble edge of the island. I hit the floor and could not breathe. I broke three ribs.

Don't be fooled by height. I fell from two stories and was able to walk away. I fell two feet and broke three ribs. Pay close attention to your work area. Move on and off your ladder with caution.

CLEAN UP

(Quick & Easy) Picture

Most people hate to clean their tools. Some people dislike it so much that they'll throw them away rather than clean them. I do not recommend throwing them away. Cleaning tools is simple if you know the professional way to do it. I have seen people working very hard making the clean up process far more difficult then need be.

Looking back into the history of paint can help us understand the cleaning process more clearly. Prior to the introduction of latex, house paint, and the later introduction of 100% acrylic paint in the late 1950s, house paint was all oil-based. Oil-based tools needed to be cleaned with paint thinner or turpentine. This solvent is flammable and odoriferous. The solvent had to be contained and used sparingly. Painters developed a *three-wash* system. This allowed them to wash tools a number of times using the same solvent. Three separate containers were used to hold the solvent, first, second and third wash respectively.

The first wash would naturally become dirty the quickest, so after a few uses, it was put aside to let the solids settle to the bottom and it could be used again. The second wash then became the first wash, the third became the second and fresh solvent was poured to make the third wash. This system was fast efficient and very economical. Since most people do not know of this method, they try cleaning their tools in the kitchen sink, or worse, in the street with a hose. DON'T EVER DO THAT! I use the described method to clean my water-based tools for the same reasons I did with the oil-based tools. It is still the best method. I keep these three buckets at my staging/shop area. It really makes cleanup efficient, easy and it saves a lot of water.

CLEANING TIP:

Properly cleaning your brushes will require a wire brush. These are typically six inches long, one and a half inches wide and with a six inch handle. First, remove as much paint from your brush as possible into the paint can. It sounds obvious, but you would be surprised how

many people try to clean a loaded brush. Next, dunk the brush into the water with a piston-like motion. After a few dunks, place the ferrule section (the metal part of the brush) on the edge of the bucket and use the wire brush to removed any dried paint stuck on the bristles.

Continue rinsing the brush in a piston motion. Before moving over to the second wash bucket, reach your hands into the water and bend the bristles into the palm of your hand. This will release paint trapped between the bristles. Turn the bristles upward and bend them backwards, toward you. As you do this you will see the paint being released from the base of the brush. Repeat this process a number of times until you see there is no change in the consistency of the paint being removed from the brush.

Now, place the handle of the brush between the palms of your hands, keeping the brush inside the bucket just above the water level. Move your hands back and forth

creating a spinning motion. There is a tool called a *spinner* which will do this, but unless you are painting on a daily basis, you really don't need it. Your hands will work just fine.

Now you are ready to go to the second wash. By the time you get to the third wash, your brush will be clean. I clean brushes first, then roller sleeves, then roller frames and grids. To spin a roller sleeve, use a clean roller frame. Make sure it is fully inside the bucket and spin the roller with your hand. When doing this, have the roller sleeve inside the bucket with the frame section on the outside.

FYI: I use 5 gallon buckets with about 2 gallons of water in them for tool cleaning. You will have to buy these buckets, but it is well worth the expense, trust me!! You can always find other uses for them.

"The way to get started
is to stop talking and
begin doing."

– Walt Disney

10

TOOLS AND MATERIALS

This may be one of my favorite chapters. Why? I LOVE TOOLS! I have tools in my box that I have had since I started my career. I even have old color decks from the 60's! OK, I may be a bit strange in that regard, but quality tools are essential to achieving a quality finished product. NEVER think you are saving money by buying cheap tools. You will fight them from start to finish and end up totally frustrated. Think of that shopping cart that has a bum wheel and won't go straight. No fun right? Quality tools do half the work for you. I have no stock in any tool manufacturer, so I have nothing to gain by pushing any particular brand. I will repeat this one more time. QUALITY TOOLS DO HALF THE WORK FOR YOU! Invest in them and you will be glad you did.

Let's talk about a paint brush...

When you put a quality brush into your paint, it absorbs the paint and holds it there until you place it onto the surface and begin to move the brush. As you begin to apply pressure a good brush will release the paint evenly and smoothly. It is much like smoothing soft butter on a fresh piece of bread. Of course it also helps if you are using quality paint. I will discuss that later. The same holds true with roller sleeves. Ask the salesperson where you buy your tools, to show you the best they have. It may cost you a little more up front, but it will be well worth it. These tools cleaned properly will last you many years and can be used again and again.

Brush Tips:

- <u>Walls:</u> Use a 3" Wall Brush. Do not use a *sash* or *angled* brush.

- <u>Trim and Doors:</u> Use a 2 1/2" or 3" sash or angled brush.

- <u>Smaller Trim Areas and Sash Windows:</u> Use small Sash Brushes.

To Tape or Not to Tape...

I see instructional books, magazines and videos that recommend applying tape to all your trim and ceiling. They recommend you do this in order to cut in the walls. They also suggest you apply tape to your walls to paint your trim. I have been painting for over 30 years and I have NEVER seen professionals apply paint using this method. I understand it may seem like it is easier for a beginner but in reality it creates more problems than it solves. I should mention many people who apply paint today use tape because they spray everything including interiors.

I don't agree with this method. It's a method used in production painting, not professional custom painting. Once again, true professionals do not use tape to cut clean corners. I recently had a custom home builder ask me if I would like to start painting his homes. I replied absolutely. He then asked me if I have a large masking crew. Masking crew? I looked at him as if he was an alien. I really couldn't believe what I was hearing. I replied NO... I have a highly skilled paint crew. As a result, we never did any business together and I am just fine with that. I believe when painting walls, it cost more for time and materials to apply the tape, remove it and then clean up the mess under the tape. The only place you should apply tape is to the baseboards to protect them from roller spatter. When you put a loaded brush against tape, paint will almost always seep under the tape, damaging the surface below. You also run the risk of lifting off the paint finish when you remove the tape.

CUTTING INTO CORNERS

Let's say the ceiling is complete and we are going to paint the walls. Load your brush with paint and paint a horizontal line about one half inch from the ceiling. Do this for as far as you can safely reach. With the paint that is on the wall, put pressure on your brush creating a straight edge with the bristles. Now work the brush up into the corner. Start moving the brush along the corner. Always keep your eyes ahead of the brush. This makes it possible to paint a straight line. Keeping your eyes focused on where you are headed when painting is the same as when you are driving a car. You keep your eyes ahead, not on the hood. Just remember to watch where your brush is headed not where it is. This may take some practice, but you will get the hang of it soon and will be painting like a pro in no time.

ROLLER PANS

In all the years I have been painting. I have NEVER used a roller pan. I have never seen any professional painter use a roller pan! Why would you want to use a method which is not common practice for professionals? You'll need to keep refilling them, they tip easily, and they are difficult to move. You have to bend completely over to reach them and they can easily fall off the ladder ledge.

I can go on and on about why I do not use them. Again, if true professionals don't use them, why would you?

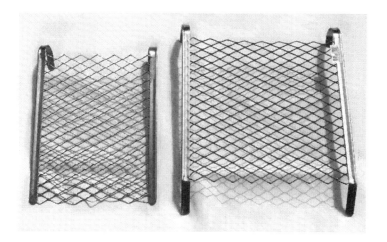

So, what do I use in lieu of a roller pan? I use buckets and roller grids. In large rooms, I use a five gallon bucket

with a five gallon roller grid and a nine inch roller. In smaller rooms like bathrooms and kitchens, I use a *deuce* (trade name for a two gallon bucket). I use a two gallon roller grid with the two gallon bucket and a seven inch roller. This is what professional painters use and I highly recommend them.

PROGRESSIVE TOOLS

There are a number of progressive tools on the market today which will claim to make your painting go faster, increase efficiency, and make clean up a snap. As I pointed out in the previous section, you can use these items if you so choose, but I have never seen any pro use these tools.

There was a time when paint was applied only with a brush. When rollers came along, they were not allowed in production work because they applied paint too fast. The same holds true for airless paint sprayers. I remember a time when you could not use them on a union project.

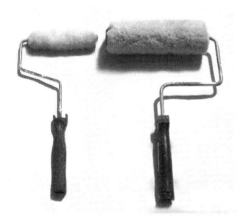

I was a kid but I remember. In my opinion those are the only inventions in my lifetime that have actually contributed to the speed, ease and efficiency of painting.

True professionals use means and methods that will produce the best results in both time and quality. Why would you do anything different?

ROLLER POLES

I have watched so many instructional videos and TV programs where they show the person painting holding the roller frame by the handle, or using a roller pan while standing on a ladder. Pros don't do it this way. Not only is it more difficult, but dangerous as well. The less time you spend on a ladder the better. Invest in a quality roller pole. They come in all sizes and are adjustable. I have a 1 – 2 ft. adjustable, a 2 – 4 ft. adjustable, a 4 – 8 ft. adjustable and a 6 - 12 ft. adjustable. For most home projects, a 2 – 4 ft. and a 4 – 8 ft. will reach most areas. If you will be working in tight areas use a 1 – 2 ft. It is much easier on your hands and your back. Seriously, never paint by holding onto the roller handle. You can thank me later.

AIRLESS SPRAYERS

I don't feel it is necessary to spend much time on production tools such as sprayers since most of you will not be using them. I am against using paint sprayers for the use of painting interior walls. I do not like the finish and it makes touching up later very difficult because the texture is different. Airless sprayers do work well for painting the ceiling and exterior of your building. There are some inexpensive sprayers on the market which I have never used so I cannot make comment on them. Many home centers and professional paint stores rent contractor grade spray equipment.

Depending on your painting requirements, the value of either one will be a personal choice.

PAINT

Finally, I can talk about paint! I have seen many changes in the painting industry in my career. Without getting into the formulation history, government regulations, variety of manufacturers etc., there is one important point I want to make about paint. ONLY USE THE HIGHEST QUALITY PAINT! Every manufacturer makes several different grades of paint. The same name-brand manufacturer makes paint for jobs ranging from production homes to high end.

The phrase, "you get what you pay for," is never truer than when it comes to coatings. After 30 years in the business, I know what I'm talking about. I can't tell you how many times I have gone to a paint store where they don't know me and the salesperson recommends a cheaper grade of paint. I ask them why? They always have the same answer, "Because it's cheaper." My reply is always the same, "It's a lesser quality right?" Of course it is and I refuse to use it. It does not go on the surface as well. It does not cover as well and it certainly won't last as long.

Labor is the most expensive component of any job so why would I risk the quality I promise my clients to save a few dollars? I won't. I am not kidding. The difference between the highest grade of paint and a medium grade is only a few dollars per gallon. Why would you use anything less than the best?

All of these different grades of products have their proper application. In your home or place of business, use only the best. Do your homework. Before you set out to buy paint, or hire a contractor, look up which manufacturer you want to use and find out which product line is their best. That's what I do.

Note: Not all home centers carry the highest grade paint from the manufacturer. Again, if this is important to you, and I hope it is, research your products.

CUSTOM COLORS VS. STOCK COLORS

The amount of stock colors each manufacturer carries will vary slightly. The color you choose will almost always be a custom color. Stock colors are generally neutral colors and deeper tones that are most popular. These colors are made in very large quantities and categorized with batch numbers. Please understand, when mixing these large batches there can be variances in the amount of colorant or other ingredients from batch to batch. The variance can make even a stock color slightly different between batches. When you are buying stock colors, be certain to check that the batch numbers match. If the numbers are different, I suggest mixing all the paint together in a large container to make all paint equal and attain uniformity. Why? Let's say your six gallons of paint is from three different batches, mixing them all together will make all your paint exactly the same as if it were all from the same batch. If all of your containers are from the same batch you do not need to mix them together. The reason for doing this is so your paint will match when you have to touch up areas of the project.

There are a few important tips about custom colors. Custom colors are different from can to can, even when you order the same color.

When a color is custom mixed, each can is done separately in either a one quart can, one gallon can, or a five gallon bucket. There are three things that could cause color variance:

1. Different batch numbers
2. Can fill quantity
3. Variance in colorant dispensed by the machine

If you are buying more than one gallon of paint with the same color for your project, always, always mix all of the paint together before using. You cannot return custom colors so do not leave one out of the mix thinking you may not need it. Mix them all together to ensure uniformity.

APPLYING CUSTOM COLORS

Instructional videos frequently teach applying paint with roller first, then going back to cut in the corners. While this may be fine for stock colors and production work, I don't recommend it for custom colors. Why? When you are using a custom color, colorant can sometimes separate. If the paint sits for a while it could affect the color. Cutting in after rolling is going to present a number of problems…especially if the cut-in area is about 4 - 5" (which is what most people do). Cutting in this way can show a variation of color and a line of demarcation. This is not a good look.

Another problem can be created when you roll the wall first. If you roll the wall first you run the risk of touching or damaging the wall while working on the cut in. You do not want to do any unnecessary touch up. When you cut in the corners, do it before you roll. That way you can get the roller close to the corners minimizing the transition from a brushed texture to a roller stipple. This is the professional way to paint.

TOUCHING UP CUSTOM COLORS

Due to colorant separation, touching up a custom color is almost impossible. You will almost always see where you touched it up. In some cases, you may have to paint the wall corner to corner in order to touch up properly. When using a custom color always buy a little more than you think you may need.

TOUCHING UP ENAMEL

(Satin-Sheen, Semi-Gloss & Gloss)

The higher the gloss level, the more difficult it is to touch up. The rule of thumb is, "You cannot touch up enamel." There are some locations such as baseboards and the lower portion of door frames or doors with texture which can be touched up, but even then you can notice the blemish. If you want to touch up an enamel surface, I recommend painting corner to corner or edge to edge. It is more work but it is just the way it is.

"There are painters who transform the sun into a yellow spot, but there are others who, thanks to their art and intelligence, transform a yellow spot into the sun."

– Pablo Picasso

"Anyone can paint,
but not everyone
can be a painter."

– Anonymous

11

DEALING WITH ARTISTS & CONTRACTORS

Most of you reading this may not want to take it upon yourself to do your own painting. You may want to hire a painting contractor. There are generally four kinds of painting contractors in the business today: competent, incompetent, licensed and unlicensed. Hiring an unlicensed painting contractor is risky business. There is even a risk hiring a licensed contractor but let's address the unlicensed ones first.

The only reason you would consider an unlicensed person is to save money. Is it worth it? I prefer not calling them a contractor because unless they have a license (at least in California) they are not a contractor. Contractors are required to be licensed, bonded and carry liability insurance. If they have employees, they need to carry workers' compensation insurance. If you hire an unlicensed person, you are exposing yourself to the following risks:

- If they damage your home in any way, you may be responsible.

- If you are unhappy with the work, or they do not complete the project, you may not have any recourse.

- If they or any of the workers get hurt on your property, you may be responsible.

Keep in mind, even if you get a bid from a licensed contractor, you will still need to check with the contractors' board to make sure they are in good standing with the board, read any claims against them and verify if they carry workers' comp insurance and which insurance company covers them. The contractors' board does not have record of liability insurance. Ask your contractor to supply a certificate of insurance. If they refuse or fail to give proof of insurance, chances are they do not have it. Also at the time of a contract they should also provide you with what is called a "Notice to Owner." This outlines your rights within the contract. Not all states have the same requirements. Check with your state to ensure you are protected.

CLASSIFICATIONS

Each respective trade has its own classification. For example, California Painting and Decorating contractors carry C-33 classifications. Drywall contractors have a D-9 classification. Roofing contractors have C-39 classifications. General contractors have a B-1 and can only perform the trades for which they hold a license. So, for example, if your general contractor does not hold a C-33 license, by law they are required to hire a licensed Painting (C-33) contractor.

They also have to be performing a minimum of three disciplines on a project to lawfully hold a contract. For example, a general contractor can not lawfully contract a project to change your roof and paint the exterior unless they hold a license for those trades.

If you live in California you can go to the contractors' board website to learn about your rights when hiring a contractor. You can search for your contractor either by company name, or by their personal name. Go to: www.cslb.ca.gov or call: 1-800-321-2752. Check your state website for information on how to obtain this information where you live.

A licensed contractor can not compete with people that are working illegally. Protect yourself by hiring a licensed contractor. It is not a guarantee the work will be performed any better, but at least you are better protected if something does go wrong. And it's the law.

Please help support those contractors that are doing things the legitimate way. We all work hard to obtain the proper credentials to offer our services lawfully.

REFERENCES

Aside from checking on a contractor through the CSLB (Contractors State License Board), asking for references is the next most important guideline to follow. If your contractor was not referred to you, ask them for referrals and call those referrals. If possible, go by some of their projects and inspect their work. It is much better to do this leg work before finding out after it's too late. Just because a contractor has a license, insurance, proper credentials and attractive marketing material, does not mean they are capable of producing quality and/or professional work. Check their history.

HOW MUCH???

When you are comparing estimates, there are a few obvious things to consider; others may not be so easy to detect up front. Contractors vary in experience level and dedication to their craft. In general what sets estimates apart from each other is dedication to the craft. Will they do it right the first time? To acquire work, many contractors need to cut corners to save you money so their proposal will be accepted. This can encompass cheaper materials, eliminating necessary procedures and less than professional looking application methods.

Some contractors survive by creating a large volume of work. They are doing so much work that if they lose on a few projects, they will not go under. Smaller contractors do not have this buffer zone so every project has to balance out. The contractor's financial position and their dedication to the craft will determine your estimate.

My goal is quality first. I love this trade. If I am not happy with the work we do, it's just not worth it for me to risk my reputation. I will walk away from a potential project if quality is not as important to the client as it is to me. Here's a quick story to further explain my point. I once had a prospective client ask me, before I even reviewed the project, if I had brought my eraser? I knew what he was alluding to but I went along and asked him why? He said, "To adjust your price." Immediately I knew I wasn't going to get the job. I didn't want it now. Why not? Because he was more concerned with the price than with the quality of work I will provide. I was referred to this person from a loyal client. I told him I do not need to adjust my price because my estimate reflects my work. I do it right the first time. We did get along on a personal level as he and his wife spent an hour talking to me about their family. They also broke out the family photo albums. I sent them my proposal knowing I was only sending it in good faith.

There are always those that are trying to make a quick buck but, I would like to think there are many other contractors that follow my same principles. When comparing prices between contractors, be sure to ask about difference in price bids. The lowest bid is low and the highest bid is high for a reason. Be aware of an estimate that is vague. Never assume everything is included. Many contractors will submit a low price to get the job and then use change orders or additional work authorizations to bring the total job cost up. It's in your best interest to know all the details. Don't be afraid to ask questions. It's your responsibility to know why. It's better to investigate in the beginning, than to be sorry in the end.

WORKING WITH ARTISTS

Working with artists is where you can enter in to muddy waters. Why? Because most artists are not contractors and most contractors are not artists. Yet quite often you will see them both representing one another. I can say this with certainty because of my experience in the business. I have worked with many talented artists but the fact is they are not contractors. I have worked with and know of many contractors that offer faux and decorative finishes, yet they definitely are not artists. Most artists went from painting canvas to painting walls with no experience in the traditional painting trade. And most contractors looking for ways to increase business added faux finishes to their list of services with little to no experience in the field of faux and decorative arts.

Here lies the problem. You have artists who are not licensed to contract painting projects so they do not carry proper insurance, workers comp etc. Bottom line, you are not protected. Then you have licensed painting contractors who do not have the proper experience of an artist putting you at risk of poorly executed finishes. So what do you do? That is what this section is about. It is not my intention to defame neither contractors nor artists but to point out their differences so you can make an informed decision. If you decide to hire these people, you become the contractor. You are responsible.

Be aware of the licensed painting contractor that also offers faux finishes. Many of these contractors know little in the way of true faux and decorative finishes. Others will subcontract this service to an artist. In either case, always check references. Be sure your contractor/artist understands color, design, and is capable of a variety of techniques. See that they have the experience to prove it. Ask to see samples and photos. Call their references and go see their work if possible. They may have learned a few finishes from a video and now sell this as part of their menu. Knowing one or two finishes does not constitute an accomplished faux finisher or decorative painter. Using a product that is similar to painting by numbers is not the work of a faux artist. Well, they could be considered a faux, faux artist. Seriously though, there are many great artists and many great contractors, but the combination of the two is very rare. With that in mind, you are now better prepared to hire a contractor or an artist. I would bet many do not know the difference between a faux finish and a decorative finish. After reading this book, you do!

Dear Dino,

I would like to thank you for the great job you did on all of the projects we've worked on together. Your professionalism and attention to detail are truly to be admired, in today's industry those are rare characteristics. My clients and I are very fortunate to have a contractor with your level of experience and expertise. You have elevated the quality of my projects to a level that I had hoped for. I look forward to working with you on many more projects in the near future.

Sincerely,
Patrick Flanigan
Patrick H. Flanigan & Associates

12

PREPARING A HOME FOR SALE

I have been improving property my entire career. Many times my clients were either realtors or their customers. I learned quite a bit in my early days about how to prepare a property for sale. I also learned how to help new homeowners transform their houses into personalized homes. This chapter will offer some proven tips that will help prepare your property for sale. It will also utilize some of the information that was presented in previous chapters.

HOME BUYERS ARE LOOKING FOR AN EMOTIONAL CONNECTION TO THEIR NEW HOME

While square footage, quality schools, parks, amenities and affordability are significant considerations when buying a home, the first impression is critical. For a buyer to want your home, they need to feel an emotional connection to it. The challenge is in knowing how to create that connection. That is what this chapter will cover.

I have theme painted rooms where some realtors said the house will never sell. They advised painting the room neutral. Much to the realtor's surprise, those very rooms were what actually sold the house. This demonstrates that you do not have to make your home neutral to appeal to everyone. Although you do need to make sure that whatever it is you have done, or plan to do, is done well. It must have harmony and be authentic.

Make your house look as good as possible. Color, furniture placement, lighting, cleanliness and functionality weigh heavily on the emotional connection. Homes which have been poorly designed or are dated need help in order to draw attention away from their negative aspects.

The idea is to direct people's attention towards the positive elements. Identify these areas and do all you can to attract attention to them. If your home is small, move out any oversized pieces. Do all you can to make the space appear as large and spacious as possible.

Is your decor dissonant? Like a song with a flat note? Are you collecting knickknacks? Is every inch of wall lined with pictures and art? Are there toys all over the house? Remember, many times your normal living conditions are not favorable to selling conditions. It is time to clear the clutter. Remove as much as possible to streamline and create continuity.

This may come as a shock to some. But trust me on this. Buyers are NOT interested in your stuff. They are trying to picture their life in your home. It is in your best interest to create an environment which showcases the home and remove anything that is a distraction from that. Focus on all of the positive aspects. Unless you come with the house, keep as much of your life's clutter out of view as possible. As I pointed out in earlier chapters: less is more.

If your home needs to be painted, paint it. Fix as many items as you can afford to repair. Present your home in pristine condition, no matter how old it is. I suggest staying away from large replacement items such as counter tops and flooring unless they are beyond reconditioning. You will be surprised how much of a transformation can be achieved by just clearing clutter and freshening up the paint.

Painting in a smart way and properly lighting your home creates an inviting atmosphere as well. Many will look past the big ticket items if your home looks clean, in good condition and feels like home the minute they walk in. If the prospective buyers can see themselves living in the home and dealing with big items later, then you are ahead of the game. Let them go through the hassle and expense of changing everything. Chances are they will want to pick their own materials anyway. If it comes down to being a deciding factor, you can always negotiate the price. At least you will save yourself time, money and inconvenience in the long term.

If all this feels like it's out of your league or over your

head to tackle, consult your realtor. They deal with this sort of thing daily. They may also work with designers that specialize in staging homes. This comes with a cost but if your home needs help, and you feel like you do too, it may be an option worth considering. Your goal is to sell your home quickly and for maximum market value.

EXTERIORS

Creating an environment to live in is extremely important but let's not forget one very important fact: people do judge books by their covers! Your property's curb appeal provides a first impression. Make it a good one. If your prospective buyer pulls up to your house and doesn't want to get out of the car, you lose. The last thing you want is to lose their interest before they get to the door. It could be perfect inside but no one may ever know because they cannot get past the look of your exterior. A poor looking exterior is a prospective buyer's first tip that they will have to shell out even more money. Most people like turn-key properties. Make your exterior presentable, otherwise they may just drive away. As I have been saying throughout this book, paint is the most economical way to transform your home. Your exterior is no exception.

Composing a color palette which is harmonious with the architecture, building materials and surrounding environment, will make your property a structure of elegance and sophistication. Attention to detail such as landscape and minor repairs is also important. If there appears to be too many necessary repairs, most people won't want to be bothered. The only thing that could change their minds is substantially discounting your price. If you are willing to do this, you need not worry about fixing things up. Always put yourself in the buyer's position.

Would you pay full price for your home in its current condition? Or would you want a discount to make the necessary repairs?

The bottom line here is to do all you can to give your home curb appeal. Do not let the condition of your exterior cause anyone to drive away without even seeing the interior.

BUYING A HOME OR DISTRESSED PROPERTY

If you have read this book in it's entirety you should be fully aware of all the possibilities at your fingertips for improving your property. This knowledge can be an asset when viewing property for either a place to call home or purely an investment. Knowing what to look for and how to make a transformation will enable you to make the best of any situation.

The benefits of your newly learned design abilities will also make your experience far more rewarding and profitable. Being able to identify areas which most likely could be deemed undesirable are your bargaining chips. You can now see the potential when others cannot. This is where you will excel. Do not let anyone (sellers in particular) in on your vision. I know this seems obvious, but sometimes when the lights go on, we get excited and want to share it with others. Don't. You will give away your advantage.

Many walk away from a good purchase because they lack the knowledge and vision to create a personalized environment with color and finishes. Sure, there are going to be situations where you will need to do much greater renovation to bring a property up to its full potential. Knowing what you have learned in this book will give you a few extra golden nuggets to work to your advantage.

You can walk into a property and start to see it in a completed form. You will see ways to make it your own personalized environment. If it will be an investment, you now have the knowledge to make the right amount of improvements to make the property appealing to others. Your goal is to turn it around for as little investment as possible. This will help you make the maximum profit. Many uninformed investors make the mistake of going overboard with remodeling. They end up unable to recover their investment. Knowing the information in this book will help you make good design decisions.

Before

During this kitchen remodel we chose tumbled stone and custom hand painted tiles by Danny Montes. The brick arch is distracting and feels heavy in the room. I decided to soften this by covering it with plaster.

After

The lightly aged plaster with subtle breakaway locations exposing the bricks soften the feel and look of the brickarch while allowing the hand painted tile to now become the focal point.

*Sometimes it's difficult to control my love
for my work*

WRAP UP

It is my sincere desire that the information in this book will help open up a new world of working with color and special finishes. Over the years I have had many experiences and been rewarded over and over with so many things money can't buy. I am extremely passionate about my craft and I love sharing it with others. The things I treasure the most are the moments I have shared with my clients. I am always thrilled when they are delighted with the results, but I also cherish the relationships that are developed and the discoveries in design we shared together. Those discoveries are now a part me and found throughout this book.

I have been fortunate to have worked alongside of many great and talented artisans over my career. They have contributed to this book through me. In turn, I hope that I have contributed to those that have worked alongside of me. It is deeply rewarding to see the lights go on in painters' eyes, or my clients' eyes when a new discovery hits them. I am honored when someone that came to me early in their career moves on to start their own business. I love to teach and help people learn about this wonderful world of color and finishes. These are the reasons why I wrote this book. Sure, I love stepping back when I am finished to see what I created. That's the other side of what I do. But it really doesn't mean much to me unless I see my client and the people working beside me just as happy. If you have read this book and feel inspired, if you have learned just one thing, and if what you have learned will help improve your life in anyway… then and only then will I be happy with this book.

ACKNOWLEDGMENTS

My career could never have been as amazing as it is without the many people that have mentored and believed in my ability. The most important person in all of this is of course my father Chuck Fauci. Although my father taught me the basics of the trade, it was his teaching of work ethic that meant the most to me. I take pride in all that I do because of him. He told me early on that regardless of what I am doing, be it sweeping a floor to painting a grand palace, be the best at it. No job is too small not to be proud of it. He also taught me discipline, honor and respect. These are the valuable tools which I use to navigate my career. It was my father who brought me to Craig Duswalt's Rock Star seminar which inspired me to write this book. Thank you Dad!

I am eternally grateful to the fine craftsman that also built upon my fathers teaching such as Stan Conoway, his brother Glenn Conaway, Henry Sammeter, Mario Ruedas, Bob Burnett and Steve Capparo. I could write a book just on my experiences with these people. Stan not only taught me painting techniques but also the art of being on time. Back when I was in high school, I was meeting Stan at the shop one morning to carpool to the job site. We were meeting at 6:00am. I arrived at 6:05am and Stan was not there. I thought that maybe he had forgotten to meet me. When I got to the jobsite, I asked Stan why he wasn't at that shop earlier. He said that he was there waiting. I told him I was there at 6:05. He said, "I told you 6:00, and if you are riding with me, I'm not waiting for you. Be on time." This was a great lesson for me. I also want to thank my brother Michael Fauci, Bob Rosenthal (Uncle Bob), and Jerry Brown for teaching me how to hang wallpaper, commercial wall coverings and fabrics. These are the guys that all helped shape my skills in so many ways.

It was John Hazelwood who first taught me the basics of faux and decorative finishes. John Hazelwood is a master and was clearly ahead of his time. He was a great teacher. Thank you John.

Thank you Rob Carlson (Carlson Art and Woodwork). You introduced me to many wonderful clients and fun projects. Rob is an amazing artist and craftsman. He also writes some great Bluegrass music!

I am also grateful to the people at Walt Disney Imagineering that believed in my ability. Jack Plettinck for asking for me to join the Animal Kingdom team, three years after we first talked in Florida. To the executives that helped me so much in Japan. Art Kishiyama, Craig Russell, John Verity and Jim Thomas. Thank you, Joe Kilanowski, for your call to lead the character paint effort on the greatest project of my life, Tower of Terror in Tokyo. It was such a great team and an amazing project. You and the entire team designed a magnificent structure. I am in awe of your talent. Most importantly you have become a treasured friend!

Thank you Craig Duswalt, Lex Gable and Karl Meinhardt and Dawn Teagarden for helping me turn this book into a reality. Your input, guidance and support are valued more than you know.

There are far too many people to mention. If I have worked with you, if you are in my life, then you have contributed to my life. Thank you!

A message from Chuck Fauci

From as young as I can remember I have been around art that my family had created (sculptures, paintings, wall creations, etc.)

My grandfather was a sculpture artist in Sicily and painted artwork in the church. He brought some of his work to the U.S., and as a boy I enjoyed it around me.

My father was a master painter. Not only could he transform a painted wall into a grained piece of art or wall paneling, he never left a home that was remodeled without painting a wall of stone and marble.

Over the years I learned from him. When I started my painting business the art I had learned got me into the life of the client. Many times I was surprised by how much I had learned in wall art, color matching and the coordinating of fabrics with it.

You have now taken our family's profession and talent to a new level. I remember looking at your project in Japan for Disney. I was awed by the many forms of stone and aging you had created. I had to walk in pretty close to realize I was looking at paint and not the real thing.

Your work now excels all of the family before you. I am very proud of you, not only for staying at my side and learning, but because you have gone on even further on your own to explore new art for your future customers.

With Love,
Dad

"When people ask me if
I like to paint? My answer is
always NO...

I love to paint!"

– Dino Fauci

TESTIMONIALS

"You can't imagine the joy and delight that your beautiful artistry has given us. It is all so gorgeous. I can't thank you enough!"

– Dixie Carter

"My husband and I purchased a brand new 4700 sq. ft. production home. The home has a "Spanish" feeling with 11 arches in the hallways and large arches flanking the main rooms. Here is where Dino excelled. He coordinated every color in every room so that the house flowed and didn't feel out of context with the rest of the colors in the house. Many rooms were painted with 3 - 4 colors, and many architectural details were faux finished to make them "pop." All the arches were painted with a faux travertine block that resembles Castle Archways. They're awesome and most people think we actually installed stone! Each of the three fireplaces took on its own character and coordinated with its respective room. My favorite room is the dining room. Dino chose reds and creams and it's painted to resemble peeling paint and exposed plaster, from perhaps ruins in an old mansion! Fantastic!!!! In all there are 21 paint colors used in our home. In addition to the walls, he distressed, painted or stained all the cabinets in our office, dining room, wine cellar and family room. Again each cabinet has its own character relating to the room itself. He's a magician!!!!!

We were really excited to work with Dino. He's an awesome creator and color coordinator extraordinaire! He has great ideas and works within his clients needs and wishes. Both Gary and I recommend him highly and feel he has added exceptional value to our home!"

Sincerely,
Gary and Carol Heil San Diego, CA

"I first met Dino in music school years ago. It was there I realized that Dino has a tremendous collaborative style. He was never interested in forcing his own ideas on anyone but much more concerned with sharing ideas and bringing out the best in people. 20 years later, and after working with him on several of my own home projects, I can attribute that success with his ability to transfer the thoughts in my mind to the project with incredible vision. Dino was able to meet and exceed all my expectations, and has the technical skill necessary to exceed your needs."

– Brian Young (Drummer) – Fountains of Wayne

"I have known Dino Fauci since 1992 and except when he is off to some exotic location designing colors and surfaces for one of his many high profile customers, we have worked together and been friends ever since. The thing that Dino brings to color design is history. There is a cultural legacy. He is Italian and Italian design is, past and present, the most beautiful in the world. He comes from a familial line of painters and finishers that is also his legacy. He grew up knowing color in a modern day equivalent of the guild experience, and the fact that Dino has been a professional painter for all his adult life is his personal legacy. He is also a stellar human being and that may be the most important legacy of all."

– *Rob Carlson, owner, Carlson Art and Woodwork*

"Dino has the unique ability to envision, create and deliver fantasy or reality through paint! He transformed my bungalow from a place of bad design decisions into my perfect living space with just paint!"

– *Karl Meinhardt, Author*

"We are sharing our thoughts about Dino Fauci to increase the world's awareness of the magical touch he has brought into our home.

Dino came into our house and transformed what was an ultra modern design into a warm Mediterranean HOME!!

Dino's special ability to direct us and create an environment that is unique, classic and most of all WARM is exactly what we were striving for.

Our beautiful home is a masterpiece. THANKS DINO!!"

All our best!!
Mel and Nikki

I have worked with Dino Fauci closely for the past four years. During that time he has character / show painted a multitude of character façade textures and surfaces.

Beginning with Disney's Animal Kingdom at the Walt Disney Resort, Dino brought life and vibrancy to the exotic architecture of Park Central, specifically the Safari Village Facilities. His ability to work color onto complex textures and impressionistic shapes and forms is unparalleled.

Dino expanded his participation on Tokyo Disney Sea in Tokyo, Japan where he played a key role in organizing and coordinating a large group of field set decorators and paint contractors. Tokyo Disney Sea is the largest and most exotic theme park in the world and I say with certainty that Dino's hard work contributed significantly to its great success.

I hope to have an opportunity to work side by side with Dino in the future and recommend his services for any project needing talent and professionalism.

Respectfully,
John Olson

Dear Dino,

You are an artist in the field of color and texture. We had hired another designer but she just couldn't understand our needs. You listened to our desires and feelings with patience. You understood the colors we liked and made them work. Our home now flows, shadows and inspires. Our desires have truly been met.

Sincerely,
John and Judy Wallace

Throughout the course of my career I am often asked similar questions on a variety of topics. This next section is a collection of the ones most frequently asked. If you have a question not found here, please send your question to dino@dinofauci.com and I will do my best to send you an answer.

FAQs:

FREQUENTLY ASKED QUESTIONS

DESIGN

Should I match the colors of my walls to the fabric of my bedspread or sofa?

NO! Choose a color which will COMPLEMENT the fabric. The idea is to create harmony. Duplication is not harmony.

My fabric consists of several colors. Can I use one of the colors on my walls?

Yes, I recommend using the one that is used the least. Be sure your goal is to complement the fabric not distract from it.

I have so many different colors and surfaces in my space. How do I choose a color that ties them all together? Isn't a shade of white the easiest?

White may be the easiest, but not necessarily the best choice. Look at all elements and determine based on the overview, which color will work with each item. Then narrow it down. For example, are the elements of the room warm or cool, or a combination? Is there a common color in the majority of the elements? Start with these questions. This will help lead you to a wise color decision.

Can I use a different color in each room?

Absolutely, as long as each color complements the next. Remember it is like composing music. If one of the notes is wrong the song is ruined. If one room is wrong it ruins the whole job. All rooms must work together, except for a room which is totally isolated from the others.

Should I paint the door of each room to match the wall color?

NO!! The only time you would paint a trim the same as the walls is if you want to make it less noticeable. Using the same color on the doors will make the space look like a rental.

What color should I paint the ceilings?

Most commonly ceilings are painted white because it gives a clean feeling to the space. White makes the ceiling feel higher which also makes it appear larger.

Can I paint my ceiling darker than the walls?

Absolutely. This is definitely a judgment call. When creating a theme or specific look it can work. A darker ceiling can be a fun effect but does not work in every situation.

Should my trim always be some shade of white?

No, not always. In most spaces where the ceilings are white or a light color, try using the same ceiling color on the trim. Darker trim colors are appropriate to specific themes and styles. There is no right or wrong. It is what makes you feel good about your space.

I have hardwood floors. What color works best in that case?

Wood has many tones, natural and stained. In Chapter 1, recall I used the brown object to determine what colors made up that color? The same applies here. Is your wood floor more reddish or greenish? How much yellow or orange do you see? Using this process along with considering your lighting conditions will help direct you. Lay your selections on the floor and look for harmony. Affix them next to the baseboard and stand back. If it does not feel right, keep trying until it does.

PREPARATION

Can I paint over a previously painted oil-based surface with water- based paint?

Yes, but you will first need to sand and clean the existing finish. There are a number of high stick primers on the market. After applying the correct primer you can paint using water-base.

Do I need to sand a glossy or semi-glossy surface before applying paint or primer?

Yes. To ensure proper adhesion you must create what is called a tooth. This is a roughness which the new coating will be able to hold on to.

Do I need to wash the surface before painting?

Yes. Always start with a clean surface. Why would you want to paint over dirt or on a contaminated surface? Clean it first. Always.

Can I use water-base paint in bathrooms and kitchen?

Yes. Only use the highest grade paint in bathrooms. Some manufacturers have specific product lines for these rooms.

Do I need to apply tape to all the trim before painting?

The only surfaces I apply tape to are the baseboard and surfaces which could be affected by roller splatter. Why? Professional painters NEVER use tape to paint a straight line. Problems you can run into when using tape: 1) The risk of pulling paint from the surface you intend to protect. 2) Paint will almost always seep under the tape damaging the surface beneath. If the surface in question will not be affected by over-spray (roller splatter) do not tape it. Follow the instructions for cutting in chapter 10, page 180.

Do I need to apply primer before painting over dark walls with a lighter color?

Although there is much information available recommending this, I do not. It has been my experience that HIGH QUALITY paint will cover darker colors in most cases with two coats. You may save a couple dollars since most primer is cheaper than the finish coat, but you will save more than that in clean up time.

I want to paint my walls deep red, orange or purple. What color primer should I use?

A medium tone gray. Why? Many make the mistake of tinting the primer in the same hue as the finish coat. The problem here is the primer will still be in the light to medium tones. This will not help much more than just using white. Why? Deep tone colors have a clear base. What is clear base? Deep colors have less titanium dioxide, which is white and opaque. The darker the color the less titanium it has and titanium is the ingredient which gives paint hiding quality. So, clear tint base paint, like in deep, rich colors, are clear like varnish with colorant added. For this reason it takes many coats to cover itself. Highest quality materials such as Benjamin Moore's Aura line are a great choice when using deep colors.

Can I paint Oak cabinets?

Yes. You will need to prepare the surface properly first. It must be sanded, cleaned and then the appropriate primer applied followed by a high quality finish coat.

Will I still see the grain through the paint if I paint my Oak Cabinets?

Yes.

Is there anything I can do to eliminate the Oak grain prior to painting them?

Yes, but it is labor intensive. There is a product made by "Fine Paints of Europe," which can be found in many small boutique type paint stores. It can also be ordered online at finepaintsofeurope.com. This is a high-building primer with five times the filling qualities of normal alkyd primers. After drying it can be sanded smooth. The price is more than $100/gallon but will save you hours in the long run. There are other grain fillers as well. All will require sanding and priming before the finish coat is applied.

I removed wallpaper and washed the walls. Do I still need to prime?

Yes. Use oil-base primer in this case. If there is any paste residue and it is not sealed properly, you will get a crackle effect when the paint dries. Not a good look if it is not what you are going for. Glue is used to purposely create the crackle effect.

PATCHING AND REPAIRS

I have textured walls and ceilings with small nail holes to be patched. What is the best method?

Use spackling paste. Apply it directly in the hole with your fingertip. This will minimize excess patching on the surface. Before the material is completely dry, wipe the excess away with a clean, wet cellulose sponge or rag. This method will usually eliminate the need to re-texture the surface.

I have textured walls and ceilings with large holes to be patched. What is the best method?

In both cases, when dry wall patch is needed to fill the hole or when patching compound will do the trick, you will need to match the texture before painting. Most texture styles can be emulated using a spray can texture found in most paint and home improvement stores. Make sure to feather the texture. What does this mean? As you move your spray texture from the center of the patched area to the previously existing area, it is important to blend into the area and not have an over buildup. You want the patch to be as seamless as possible.

I have large holes in my moldings, trim and doors. Can I use "Bondo" (polyester resin) to repair them?

Yes. Most paint and home improvement stores carry Bondo. It is an all purpose putty. This is a two part material which is very toxic. Wear a protective mask when using this material. Make sure the area to be patched is clean and dust free. I recommend priming the area before applying Bondo.

Can I paint directly over Bondo or other patching materials without first applying a primer?

NO!

My drywall has cracks from settling or an earthquake. Can I just fill the crack with patching material?

You can, but it will not last. The method I use takes time but will yield the best results. First locate the studs closest to the cracked area. Using drywall screws and a power screwdriver, secure the drywall on both sides of the crack. Do this at every possible stud. Optional Step: Cut away surface paper of the existing drywall to allow for new fiberglass tape and patching compound. Prime the paper area with a quick-dry primer. Apply fiberglass tape and joint compound. Do not use topping compound. Patch the area until the tape is covered. Apply texture to match. By securing the drywall to the studs, it will prevent the drywall from moving.

PAINT QUALITY

I read that a certain brand is rated the best above all others. Is this really the best brand?

Most likely it is the best amongst the ones it was tested against. Almost every paint manufacturer offers a number of different grades of quality, typically 3 to 4 choices. This is to satisfy a wide range of requirements and preferences. There is a difference, trust me. I have found most major home improvement centers do not generally carry the highest quality material available from the product line. If you have a favorite brand, ask for information on ALL of their products so you can make the best choice.

APPLICATION

I received a quote for the interior painting of my house. The contractor wants to spray everything. Is that a good option?

The only reason to spray is to save on cost. I do not like sprayed finish unless it is followed by a procedure called back-rolling. Why? The paint has to be watered down to spray. The finish is difficult to touch-up later. Spraying can also leave spray-lines (overlap marks created by the spray mist).This is a production method of painting and I am strongly against it. If cost is an issue, it may be a consideration. Get a few bids from several contractors comparing prices and methods of application.

Should my interior trim, doors, etc., be sprayed or painted with a brush?

This depends on your overall design. With modern or contemporary, a sprayed method is widely desirable. If your design is more traditional or old world, there is nothing more appealing than a professionally hand painted brush finish to make your design authentic. NOTE: There were no sprayers in the Old World!

Should I cut-in with a brush first or roll the walls first?

Cut-in first! Why?

1. *If you decide to roll first, you run the risk of damaging the finish by touching, leaning on, or brushing up against it.*

2. *If you are using a custom color, you will run the risk of seeing brush marks.*

By rolling first, you can get the roller tight against the corners, minimizing brush marks. Colorant settlement in custom colors increases the chance of brush and roller differences not to mention texture differences. Cut-In first and avoid these problems.

GLOSSARY

Acid Stain: Chemical used to stain (color) concrete.

Acoustic Ceiling Coating: Also known as *Popcorn Ceiling,* or *Cottage Cheese Ceiling,* is a mechanically sprayed on coating used to provide acoustic benefits to rooms, or absorb sound. It also was used to reduce construction costs.

Aging: A series of techniques used to create the *oldness,* well-used or weathering effects with the use of paint.

Arches: Can be structural or decorative. Typically found in European and Middle Eastern architecture.

Back Splash: This is the area behind a sink where the counter meets the wall. A back splash is usually made from a waterproof material such as stone or tile to protect the wall from becoming damaged. This can be a decorative element as well as a protective one.

Base Coat: When painting a specialty finish, a base coat is the final coat prior to the application of the specialty treatment. The term Base Coat is quit often used to describe a prime coat, which is incorrect. A prime coat in most cases is necessary before a base coat can be applied.

Blend: To smooth a material (paint) until no point of application is visible, i.e. no starting or ending point.

C-33 Classification: Painting and decorating license classification for the State of California.

Cat Face Plaster: A design created by manipulating plaster or drywall mud to create recessed or undulated texture in a surface. The finished look can appear as a cat face.

Character/Theme Painting: Paint techniques used to create specific surfaces and to recreate the effects of weathering and aging while adding historical character to architecture.

Clear Coat: This material is a clear varnish, urethane or acrylic coating designed to protect the surface to which it is applied. It is also used to enhance or diminish the gloss of a finish. For example: Many decorative and character wall finishes require a flat appearance so a *clear flat* coating is used. Most faux marble requires a gloss finish to help bring out the depth of the multiple layers and add to the authenticity.

Color Chip: A color sample from the paint manufacturer or self-produced color samples.

Color Fan Deck: A stack of paint color sample strips attached together to make a stack which can be fanned out. It is the full spectrum of colors available from the respective paint manufacturer. Most decks will start with the darkest of every color and gradate towards the lighter shade of that color. This is done by adding white to the original color. You will notice the bottom of each card has the darkest tone of that color and the colors get lighter as they reach the top of each page. Some color fan decks will also provide gloss examples.

Color Theory: The science and practical methods of how color is mixed (combinations of color), and how it is perceived.

Color Wash: A material created by thinning conventional paint or glaze to an almost watery consistency.

Combing: A technique of removing glaze from a surface using specific metal, plastic or rubber combs. Various patterns can be created. This is best done on smaller surfaces such as furniture, wainscot or smooth moldings.

Cultured Stone: A material created by mixing concrete, aggregate, and pigments, and, placing it in molds to simulate real stones and rocks.

Curb Appeal: The appeal of the exterior appearance of a property from the street or curb-side. If a property has curb-appeal it looks good from the street.

Cutting in: Technique using a brush to apply paint into corners, around molding and trim. This is usually done prior to using a roller to paint a wall or ceiling.

Decorative Finish: These finishes are very often referred to as a faux finishes when in fact there is nothing fake about them. Most wall and furniture treatments you see are decorative finishes. In other words, they do not emulate any real material.

Distressing: This applies to techniques used primarily on wood and metal to recreate the effects of weathering, aging and abuse. It is used on siding, trim, fences, roofs, props and more. These techniques include sandblasting, tooling (variety of tools), burning and brushing.

DIY: Do It Yourself

Enamel: Enamel paints are a hard film material. They can be, oil-based, alkyd-based (dries from the inside out making it fully cured when dry) or water-based (dries from the outside in). As a result a skin forms on the surface giving the appearance it's dry but in most cases will take up to a few weeks to fully cure. In most cases enamel paints have a shiny or glossy finish. In recent years the term *flat-enamel* has been used. This material although it does not resemble traditional enamel in appearance, is considered scrubbable and offers similar cleaning and abrasion qualities of traditional enamel.

Environmental Condition Finishes: The effect the environment (weather) has on a surface or material. It can also mean the current condition of the weather.

Fantasy Finish: Whimsical, futuristic, atmospheric finishes that playfully represent something imaginary.

Faux Artist: An artist trained in creating and applying faux finishes

Faux Finish: A finish that authentically duplicates a natural surface such as stone, marble, wood, metal, concrete, fabric, paper etc.

Film: A thin layer of material on top of another surface.

Flat (Finish): A flat finish has between 0% and 10% light reflection qualities. This varies between the product's quality and the paint manufacturer. Typically lower quality paint has less sheen due to the higher amounts of clay, cheaper pigments, resins or polymer (binders).

Grid: A metal screen placed in a bucket or pail to remove excess paint from a roller prior to being applied to a wall or surface to be painted. Used by professionals instead of roller trays.

Hard Edges: Definitive lines made by paint or other mediums that have dried before being blended to where no line or ending point is visible.

Hardscape: Landscaping material such as concrete, stones, bricks and pavers, used to create walkways, driveways etc.

Hue: Describes the distinct characteristic of color that distinguishes red from yellow from blue. These hues are largely dependent on the dominant wavelength of light that is emitted or reflected from an object.

Knockdown Texture: A mechanically sprayed on gypsum-based product usually made from drywall topping mud applied with much larger droplets than an orange peel texture. Once the mud starts to set up, a broad knife is used to knock down the mud leaving a smooth top surface with recessed areas. This method was initially used for the same reason as orange peel. However a knockdown texture hides even more imperfections and gives the appearance of a Spanish texture.

Note: Orange peel and knockdown textures are available in aerosol spray cans for small projects and repairs from most home centers and paint stores.

Layering: Thin layers of transparent material that build depth when applied over one another.

Layers: Multiple coats (usually thin) applied for specific decorative effects. Term can also describe multiple coats of paint.

Lime Base Paint: Paint formulated with slacked lime and principally inorganic pigments. Paint can be used as either a protective or decorative coating.

Material (Paint): Material can be anything other than tools, i.e. patching material, paint, texture, coating, etc.

Mist: A very fine application of water or solvent.

Negative Ragging: The wash or paint material is first applied to the surface and removed from the surface using a wet rag. The wet rag is kept in a bucket of clean water. It removes the desired amount of paint.

Old World: Term used to reference a period look from the past.

Orange Peel Texture: A mechanically sprayed on gypsum based product usually made from drywall topping mud. The finish resembles that of an orange peel. It was created to reduce the cost of a smooth wall finish in production homes.

Palette: A flat surface usually made of plastic, wood or even cardboard used to mix and blend paint prior to application.

Patina: The term patina is quite often associated with the blue-green color that occurs on copper. It can be achieved either naturally or artificially by the use of chemicals (acid). A patina is in fact, a superficial covering. It is a process that happens over time and can be aesthetically appealing. A patina can occur on a variety of surfaces. It adds character, definition and historical elegance.

Prep-Coat: Any treatment performed to a surface prior to the prime-coat, i.e. acid bath (etching) for non-ferrous metals and concrete.

Prime-Coat: Applied before any finish or base-coat can be applied. It can be of various materials compatible with the substrate and consecutive coatings.

Ragging: A technique of applying paint, glaze or other medium to a surface with a moist or wet rag.

Rag Roll (a.k.a., Positive Ragging): A paint texture created by saturating a rag into the paint and then rolling it over the surface.

Sheen: The gloss factor of a material. The amount of gloss is its ability to reflect light. In other words, how shiny it is.

- High-Gloss – Reflects more than 90% of light
- Gloss – Reflects 70 to 90% of light
- Semi-Gloss – Reflects 40 to 70% of light
- Satin/Eggshell – Reflects 10 to 20% of light
- Flat – Reflects 0 to 10% of light

Specialty Finish: This is a very broad term used to describe a multitude of various techniques. In general, anything beyond a base-coat, or beyond what is considered traditional painting.

Spritz Bottle: A bottle that includes a trigger hand pump.

Sponging: A technique of applying paint, glaze or other medium to a surface using a sponge (natural sea sponge or synthetic/cellulose).

Staging Area: Location at a jobsite where tools and equipment are stored for the duration. This is also known as a *shop*. It is basically where you set up the paint, tools and other items necessary to do the job.

Stay-cation: A stay-at-home vacation. It can be enhanced by creating a themed environment (dedicated room) in one's home.

Stenciling: Using a plastic sheet, cardboard or stencil paper in which a design or lettering has been cut. Paint or glaze applied to the sheet will reproduce the pattern on the surface beneath.

Strie: A French word meaning striated or stripes. A decorative technique used to create streaked strip appearance. It is created by using a dry brush to remove wet glaze applied freshly over a base coat. Strie should be used on a smooth surface for best results.

Substrate: A surface to be covered with a coating such as paint or other coating/covering.

Surface Texturing: The use of plaster, cement products or other mediums applied to walls, ceilings, floors and other surfaces to simulate everything from European plaster to stone, wood or metal.

Surrounds: These are architectural elements that surround such things as doorways and fireplaces.

Theme Finish: Paint techniques used to create a particular time period or style. Often they are used in theme parks and entertainment venues.

Tones, Tints, and Shades: These terms are often used inappropriately but they describe fairly simple color concepts. The important thing to remember is how the color varies from its original hue. If white is added to a color, the lighter version is called a *tint*. If the color is made darker by adding black, the result is called a *shade*. And if gray is added, each gradation gives you a different *tone*.

Tone on Tone: This consists of two sheen qualities of the same color, i.e. flat and semi-gloss layered or applied next to each other. Another situation is one color slightly lighter than the other. They can be of the same sheen or different, as long as they appear slightly different in tone.

Traditional Painting: Also know as base painting. This is the fundamental painting process of surface preparation and the application of a single color coating, stain or clear coat.

Tromp L'oeil: Painting techniques used to create an illusion of reality.

VOC: Volatile Organic Compounds: These are considered toxic gases which are released while paint dries.

ABOUT THE AUTHOR

Dino is an anomaly in the business. An artist that was fortunate enough to grow up in a contracting family. He literally has had a brush in his hand since he was three years old. From that point on there was nothing stopping him from becoming a leader in his field. His experience and range of ability is uniquely his own.

"I never imagined that working with my father would lead to such a rewarding career. I truly love what I do and greatly value the relationships I have made along the way. I feel very fortunate to have the ability and opportunity to add something special to people's lives," says Dino Fauci. His love for his work was evident early on. The trade of painting and general contracting, being a Fauci family tradition, made it easy for Dino to express his passion for painting. The love of going to work with dad was incredibly inspiring, "As a child, I chose painting over playing. I liked it that much," says Dino. When he could have been participating in summer vacation or weekend activities, the young Fauci instead was hard at work doing the activity he enjoyed most, painting.

Dino's introduction to his trade was during a time when painters were still craftsmen who took great pride in their work. The trade was respected for the art form that it is. It was a different world back then. A

"Dino at age 3 painting the house with his brother Michael"

painter studied and practiced his craft to achieve excellence in all aspects of the trade.

The men Dino was fortunate enough to work with growing up were highly skilled, old-school craftsmen. They imparted that ethic to the young boy who was so eager to learn and be the best at his trade.

This was only the beginning of an amazing journey. Dino has since enjoyed a wide range of experiences during his vast career. After mastering the skills of traditional painting and developing his natural understanding of color and textures, he was inspired to take it to another level. Faux finishing was of great interest to this passionate painter. Mastery of specialty finish techniques became his goal. Dino trained with master faux finisher John Hazelwood and is now a master in his own right. The incorporation of these skills fit perfectly into his existing business and eventually became his focus.

The love of what one does makes for a limitless future. Dino Fauci experienced this in a grand way. Walt Disney Imagineering, the absolute gold standard for faux finishing, was Fauci's next stop. As Senior Principle Production Designer, Dino developed countless finish designs and art directed hundreds of painters at four unique Disney parks in the US and Japan. Projects Fauci worked on included, Disney's animal Kingdom in Orlando, Disney's California Adventure in Anaheim, Tokyo Disney Sea in Japan and a myriad projects at the original

Disneyland in California. One project Dino is most proud of is the amazing "Tower of Terror" at Tokyo Disney. It is the largest theme painted building in the world.

"I'm inspired by color and the effect it has on our daily lives," states Fauci. Working on numerous residential and commercial projects nationwide has afforded this master faux finisher the opportunity to interact with an incredibly diverse array of individuals. "Each project brings with it different ideas and design requirements that keep me motivated," says the artist.

Developing a color palette and specific finishes which transform a home or business into a personal environment are his passion. This concept is essential in the work he does in all venues. Dino prides himself in providing not only a wonderful new look to the surroundings he transforms, but creating an emotional experience for the viewers of the space. Creating something that renews an individual's connection with their lifestyle and business, and which is appreciated on a daily basis, are the rewards that continue to inspire this amazing artist. Some notables Fauci has had the pleasure to work with are: Dixie Carter, Hal Holbrook, Babaloo (Marc) Mandel, Melody Thomas Scott, Leslie Ann Warren, Joe Mantegna, Tom House, Jonathan Kellerman, John Lloyd, Kathy Smith, William Ahmanson, Carlson Art and Woodwork, The Hollywood Bowl Museum, Extreme Pizza, Peterson Brothers and Caruso Affiliated.

Dino is available for the following:

Art Direction/Production Design

Trade Shows / Training Programs

Color Consulting

Specialty Finish Design

Construction/Remodels

For bookings please visit
the contact page at:
dinofauci.com